Delivering Impact in Management Research

Impact is of increasing importance to all researchers, given its growing centrality to those who fund, assess and use research around the world. *Delivering Impact in Management Research* sets out a detailed and nuanced analysis of how research impact is best delivered in practice. Starting with a rich conceptualisation, the authors move on to discuss models through which meaningful impact is framed and delivered. The book explains processes, skills and approaches to impact, along with examples and insights into potential pitfalls and solutions.

Examples are drawn from around the world and systems such as the UK Research Excellence Framework (REF) are discussed as part of a key contribution to primary debates globally. A significant contribution to the long-standing discussion about relevance in business, management and organisation studies research, this concise book is essential reading for scholars and university administrators seeking to advance their understanding of delivering and demonstrating world-class research that matters.

Robert MacIntosh is the chair of the Chartered Association of Business Schools and the head of the School of Social Sciences at Heriot-Watt University, UK.

Katy Mason is the chair of the British Academy of Management and a professor of Markets and Management at Lancaster University Management School, UK, where she is also an associate dean for Research.

Nic Beech is a vice-chancellor of Middlesex University having previously been a vice-principal of the University of St Andrews and the provost of the University of Dundee, UK.

Jean M. Bartunek is the Robert A. and Evelyn J. Ferris chair and a professor of Management and Organization at Boston College, USA.

**BRITISH ACADEMY
OF MANAGEMENT**

Management Impact
Series Editors: Jean M. Bartunek, Nic Beech and Cary Cooper

Scholarly research into business and management proliferates globally. Its impact into management practice can be difficult to monitor and measure. This series, published in association with The British Academy of Management, presents Shortform books that demonstrate how management scholarship has impacted upon the real world.

Incorporating case study examples and highlighting the link between scholarship, policy and practice, the series provides an essential resource for postgraduate students and researchers seeking to understand how to create impact through their work. The concise nature of the books also ensures that they can be useful reading for reflective practitioners.

Delivering Impact in Management Research
When Does it Really Happen?
Robert MacIntosh, Katy Mason, Nic Beech and Jean M. Bartunek

For more information about this series, please visit: www.routledge.com/Management-Impact/book-series/IMPACTM

Delivering Impact in Management Research

When Does it Really Happen?

**Robert MacIntosh, Katy Mason,
Nic Beech and Jean M. Bartunek**

Routledge
Taylor & Francis Group

LONDON AND NEW YORK

First published 2021
by Routledge
2 Park Square, Milton Park, Abingdon, Oxon OX14 4RN

and by Routledge
605 Third Avenue, New York, NY 10158

Routledge is an imprint of the Taylor & Francis Group, an informa business

© 2021 Robert MacIntosh, Katy Mason, Nic Beech and Jean M. Bartunek

British Library Cataloguing-in-Publication Data
A catalogue record for this book is available from the British Library

Library of Congress Cataloging-in-Publication Data
A catalog record for this book has been requested

ISBN: 978-0-367-55055-4 (hbk)
ISBN: 978-0-367-55968-7 (pbk)
ISBN: 978-1-003-09589-7 (ebk)

Typeset in Times New Roman
by Apex CoVantage, LLC

A note on authoring

We have decided to break with one performative tradition and listed ourselves in reverse alphabetical order as authors of a shared text. This is because the contents of this book can be traced to a series of discussions over many years and at many different conferences. Individually, each of us has written about research, relevance, practice and impact. Collectively, we have talked about these themes and our written outputs on them many times. Gradually, we formed the view that we had something to say and the result is this book. The ideas we present have been shaped by our conversations and, we hope, represent exactly the kind of purposeful and co-developed knowledge that we discuss in the book. As academics, we would note that the ideas presented here represent more than the sum of our individual contributions and are owned by us all, in equal measure.

Robert MacIntosh

I would like to dedicate my contributions to this book to three sets of people. First, to my beautiful wife Anne and our children Euan, Eilidh and Eva. Writing a book during a pandemic gave me the privilege of spending more time with you than would ordinarily be the case. It is fortunate, for me at least, that presented with a choice of being anywhere in the world, I would choose to be at home and in your company. Second, to my co-authors for routinely brightening my day when meeting in cyberspace to discuss this project during the strangest of years. Third, to my dearly beloved Uncle, Donald Leiper, who passed away in January 2021. He was, and will always remain, one of my heroes.

Katy Mason

I dedicate this book to my sister Vicky Pratt, mother Christine Mason, late father John Bertram Mason, brother William Mason and late sister-in-law Helen Mason, whose sadness and battle against cancer led me to management research that sought to bring better and more timely treatment and care to the sick. Like Robert, I thank my co-authors who have been, for many years, an inspiration and remain central to my intellectual life.

Nic Beech

For Linda and Rosie.

Jean M. Bartunek

I dedicate my contributions to this book first to Chris Keys, my doctoral advisor, a community psychologist whose care and concern about research mattering to people whose lives may not be easy has inspired me all through my career. Second, I dedicate it to my co-authors from whom I have learned so much to which I would otherwise be oblivious. Third, I dedicate it to the Society of the Sacred Heart, which has always modelled profound care for our world.

Contents

Illustrations

Figures

Tables

Appendix

1 Conceptualising impactful management research

This book seeks to answer a seemingly simple question. How, when and for whom does management research create impact not only on scholarship but also on practice? While we recognise multiple meanings and approaches to impact, our focus will be on impact as evidenced change in practice occurring as a result of the purposeful application of co-developed knowledge. We will argue for the importance of a relational and processual view of impact which: both delivers immediate outcomes in the context of practice and also creates value at a meta level of method and process; incorporates different kinds of knowledge to bring together analytical and practical expertise (to co-develop new knowledge); and operates ethically with a "flat hierarchy" and equity of regard for all participants. Later in this chapter, we introduce a two-level model of impact in which we explore the immediate level of a specific change, such as a new technique being introduced in a professional service firm, and a meta level in which ongoing learning resonates as the firm applies the thinking to other functional areas and the researchers adapt their methods in view of their own learning from the project. There are choices for academic experts and professional/practitioner experts, and we explore how these can be understood and so seek to assist those interested in achieving impact in developing a repertoire of impact-making knowledge with which to improvise when undertaking the exciting opportunities of impactful work.

The processes of organising and managing are central to every aspect of human life. The products and services that we access in our day-to-day activities are provided by a wide range of public, private and charitable organisations, each of which is managed in some way shape or form. Our schools of business and management house more students than any other discipline and prepare some graduates for careers leading organisations of every shape and size, whilst preparing others to form their own organisations. It seems natural then that management research matters because it is capable of reaching into every aspect of society and economy (Bastow et al., 2014).

Alongside scale and reach, we will argue that because management specifically addresses coordination, collaboration and engagement, there is an ethical drive to include management research in multidisciplinary, multistakeholder work to embed inclusivity. Management is the ideal disciplinary base to combine with arts, humanities, social sciences and sciences if they are to produce truly effective change. Equally, the matters of pressing urgency for our societies, for example, defined by the UN sustainability goals and the grand challenges we face such as health inequalities, poverty, inclusive economy, social justice and sustainability, require integrated social and sometimes socio-technical system change – the very stuff of impactful management research. For us, the connective potential of management research is simply too important to neglect if we care about improving the world.

Despite this potential for impact, our field has long been beset by concerns about relevance (see Starkey and Madan, 2001; Bartunek and Rynes, 2014) and these concerns do not seem to be resolving (e.g. Nobel, 2016). In 2017, we commissioned a special issue of the *British Journal of Management* (BJM), which attracted the highest number of submissions ever received for a special issue of that publication. BJM had previously addressed related topics on relevance and on the very nature of management research, suggesting that there remains a healthy appetite to understand and to address our discipline's place in the world. In this book, we build on the arguments set out in that special issue (see MacIntosh et al., 2017) and develop a framing of impact which goes beyond a narrow definition of research to incorporate the full range of academic activities in classrooms and curricular that includes other stakeholders such as the professions as partners in impact and that considers the temporal nature of impact as it emerges.

Impact

In everyday usage, impact is defined as the action of one object coming forcibly into contact with another. Perhaps, fortunately, there is limited evidence of peer-reviewed management research outputs coming "forcibly" into contact with policy and practice but this definition of impact privileges the idea of impact as a singular event. Our intention in this book is to present a richer conceptualisation of impact as a process and, in so doing, to move beyond a linear framing that focuses almost exclusively on the heroic but idealised cases of individual research insights which directly impact practice. Rescher (1996: 7) suggests that natural existences "consists in, and is best understood in terms of processes rather than things, of modes of change rather than fixed stabilities" and we would echo that sentiment in our view of impact as a plurivocal process through which multiple audiences are impacted in multiple ways over and through time. Therefore, **we define impact as evidenced change occurring as a result of the purposeful application of co-developed knowledge**.

We are aware that impact has been discussed in other ways (such as those we discuss later), such as in citation counts and the simple translation of academic findings for practitioners. Later in this chapter, we set out four types of impact (see Figure 1.1) and a focus on citation counts and translation would be an example of Type One. In this book, however, we set out to explore additional approaches, which have a basis in co-design and collaborative relationships between academics and practitioner experts. We will argue that each type of impact is valid, and the important thing is to overtly choose the approach that best fits the problem/opportunity at hand and to be aware of the options that are available.

In defining impact in this way, we seek to emphasise its purposeful and relational character. Sometimes, a distinction is drawn between theoretical and practical knowledge, in simple terms, the knowledge about *why* things are as they are and the knowledge about *how* to change things. Impactful knowledge combines these purposes of knowing so that analytical and normative thinking are intertwined in a learning orientation that understands and acts. The relational aspect of impactful knowledge requires different types of expertise, for example, combining analytical skills with experiential insight. If impactful knowledge is to be effectively produced and enacted these forms of expertise need to influence each other (e.g. Van de Ven, 2007), and this means that their role and status need to be explicit. Sometimes, we talk of "academics" and "practitioners" but in reality we are all practitioners, or experts, who can make distinctive contributions to a collaborative effort to produce and apply new knowledge.

In the context of impactful management research, we foreground the importance of knowledge held by a variety of actors, including those with academic expertise and those with management or professional expertise, and note that the ability to translate between and integrate across different areas of expertise is key. Different forms of knowledge can co-exist in combinations such as explicit or tacit, individual or shared and such forms of knowledge are not "subordinate to, or made up out of any other" and each form of knowledge does "work that the others cannot" (Cook and Seely-Brown, 1999: 382). Hassard and Kelemen (2002), Knorr Cetina (2010) and Van de Ven (2007) show that different experts (researchers, practitioners and policymakers) use different forms of knowledge and expertise, for example, abstract or immediately applicable knowledge in a specific context and that alternative forms of knowledge decay, transform, stabilise become institutionalised differently. We expand on these conceptualisations in Chapter 3, but note here is that this suggests the need for a flat hierarchy between alternative forms of expertise that embody, produce, use and transform knowledge.

As Usher et al. (1997: 121) observe: "Context-independent knowledge [theory] is [typically] ascribed a superior epistemological status to context-specific knowledge. This status also becomes a normative status, where context-specific practitioner knowledge is constructed as a limited and inferior form of knowledge; in effect, it is defined as not 'real' knowledge at all". We argue, in contrast, that to understand the impact well, in the broader conceptualisation that this book argues for, the traditional power and privileged position of theoretical knowledge over practical knowledge must be rebalanced and the focus should move away from a question of who *owns* which type of knowledge to a question of what each participant can *contribute* from their knowledge and expertise. The different ways of knowing do not need to be reduced so a singular approach but rather the dialogue between them can produce "arresting moments" of insight and action which produce, in turn, theoretical developments (and this is discussed further in Chapter 4).

To address our question of how, when and for whom management research might create impact, we first consider two levels at which impact occurs – the immediate and the meta. An example that illustrates this is the Fuel from Waste project (Griffiths, 2011). This project, and others like it, meets the definition of impact as collaborative effort to effect positive change in the world. Here, the purpose was to enable change for those living in areas of deprivation in Africa, reducing their reliance on charcoal fuel by producing fuel briquettes from domestic waste and in turn.

The immediate impact in this example is the application of technology to change the access to fuel. From this immediate impact, a meta level of impact flows. For example, where participants in the projects become included in the economy, setting up small businesses to sell fuel briquettes. Over time, other impacts emerge as the researchers involved reflect on how they went about the project, the particular skills needed and how they stepped outside their training to develop approaches of understanding and participating in cultures that would be more familiar to social anthropologists. In examples of this type, immediate impact is followed by a broader, meta impact in the context of the project (such as greater participation of women in an economy) and the academic context (such as development of the methods and practices which the researchers apply in subsequent projects).

In this example, impact generates three different forms of value. Firstly, there is value in the immediate context of the work, such as the implementation of technology to produce fuel briquettes. Secondly, there is value in the broader context of the work, created over time, through the broader social impacts of the initial, direct and usually deliberate outcomes of immediate impact. These could include, for example, further beneficial consequences of the immediate change, such as further use of the technology allied with support for entrepreneurial start-up, which enable people not only to heat their homes but also to set up small businesses which give them a source of income. Thirdly, there is value in the research context and process, often created by methodological developments and changes to research practice enacted in future engagements. Hence, there can be value to the academic team in rethinking how they develop their next project and to the broader academic community, for example, in how skills for impact become incorporated into doctoral training. The value derived from research may vary across particular types of stakeholders. But truly impactful work requires the skills and processes of developing all three types of value which in turn requires a rounded view of the range of participants directly and indirectly, immediately and eventually involved in delivering impact. Figure 1.1 shows these levels of impact and the associated values.

In partial answer to our opening question, impact as presented here is delivered by a broad range of participants over an extended period of time to deliver multiple forms of value to a range of stakeholders. This is in contrast to the usual ways of accounting for impact in academic systems that tend to focus on a narrower range of value which is amenable to more direct causal analysis as illustrated by Bastow et al. (2014). There are, however, signs of change. For example, Ottoline Leyser (2020), the CEO of the UK Research and Innovation (the major body that oversees the public research funding bodies for the UK universities), has argued for a systemic change of culture in research towards a collective and collaborative approach which engages people across occupations from academia and industry and from

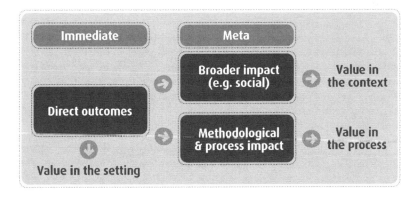

Figure 1.1 Levels of impact

less represented groups. This book will address how we might go about such a relational culture change.

Why do universities support academic research?

Bresnen and Burrell (2013) note that over the centuries, courtly, aristocratic, ecclesiastical and mercantile patronage played a role in enabling research and practice across the arts and sciences. The idea that funding shapes research agendas is important and it is, therefore, worth considering who are patrons of contemporary management research? And what do they get for their patronage? Our research is supported by our universities, by governmental funding agencies, by industry and occasionally by individual curiosity. Some argue that "disputes on the purpose and nature of management research appear to have taken on some of the characteristics of language games" (Romme et al., 2015: 545). (Although from a Wittgensteinian perspective, language games are neither trivial nor playful, but are epistemologies which are exercised within groups, similar to what can be regarded as communities of practice, and which represent a significant challenge for translation between different communities (Beech, 2008)). Indeed, one is left to wonder whether "the only real beneficiaries of the protracted debate on relevance are those academics who make short-term publishing gains" (MacIntosh et al., 2012: 374).

That said, business, management and organisation research (which we refer to hereafter, as simply management research) has expanded in scope and scale to the extent that in the UK, for example, there are over 14,000 full-time-equivalent staff in business schools with significant numbers of doctoral students, research associates and others also engaged in research. Indeed, 12% of all university students in the UK and 8% of all staff are covered by management as a subject area.

Davis notes that "judging by the number of scholars involved and their volume of research output, the field of organizational research has been an incredible success" (2015: 179). Today, many thousands of articles, papers and books are published on the subject of management every year and our industry continues to expand.

Our concern is that the measurement of impact has become too narrow in terms of immediate value and in terms of the chronology of diffusion. In the UK, public funding has created an incentive to measure impact through successive research assessment processes which we discuss further in Chapters 2 and 6. More generally, websites like the Web of Science and organisations such as Academic Analytics focus almost solely on citations and equivalent measures. There is an implicit linear, temporal sequence (i.e. impactful papers beget more impactful papers). Increasingly, visible measurement systems within the university sector mean that "scholars are now much more attuned to where, when and how they publish" (Pettigrew, 2011: 348) and academic worth is judged, in considerable part, by "how many people cite your work" (Barley, 2016: 3; also see Bastow et al., 2014). Whether through national audits of research excellence or individual audits for promotion or tenure, "the dominant metric remains citations" (Davis, 2015: 182). Yet this need to persuade a jury of sophisticated peers (McCloskey, 1998) of the merits of a scholarly publication has resulted in a situation where few practicing managers find research presented in a form that they find useful (Markides, 2011). We see scholarly publication as being of high value, but we do not see it as being the *whole* value. The typology we propose in this book, and illustrated in Figure 1.2 as a "map" of alternative types of impact, is intended to broaden the perspective on impact whilst maintaining a focus on high-quality work.

One reason for this is that it takes years of specialist training and a Ph.D. to differentiate between high-quality, rigorous research and other forms of interpretation of organisational phenomena. That is, joining the language game, which is essentially an epistemology (Wittgenstein, 1953), is more or less a full-time job. Many articles are written by academic "producers" for an academic audience that is primarily constituted by other "producers". It is perhaps unsurprising that this has not endeared us to practicing managers. As one respondent in a study noted, "the academic community is two or three cycles behind practice. We [practicing managers] are more use to them than they [academic researchers] are to us" (Beech et al., 2010: 1347). However, we would contend that while there may be different perceptions

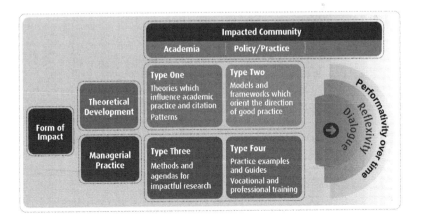

Figure 1.2 Impact map

of pace and timing between managerial experts and academic experts, in fact, many articles have a long life in influencing practice over many years. Equally, "wicked" or complex problems often require a combination of pragmatic action and rigorous analysis, pursued over time, and often including more than one type of impact as identified in Figure 1.2.

Over the same time frame as management research has been evolving towards a "productionist" view (Heusinkveld et al., 2011), the nature of both organisations and organising has changed rapidly. Entirely new industries have emerged, enabled by new technologies, and "organizations are morphing furiously into new forms" (Barley, 2016: 2). At a point where we thought organisational life could not change at a faster pace, a global pandemic has forced a large scale, social experiment with new forms of digitally enabled organising. Set against this tumultuous context, a conceptualisation of impact founded on a temporal sequence where "upstream" research impacts on "downstream" practice seems somewhat impoverished.

Publishing and management impact

A number of significant journals have curated special issues or issue sections on the nature, purpose and relevance of management research. These include the *British Journal of Management* (2001, Volume 12), the *Academy of Management Journal* (2001, Volume 44, Issue 2; 2007, Volume 50, Issues 4–5), the *Journal of Management Studies* (2009, Volume 46, Issue 3), *Organization Studies* (2010, Volume 31, Issues 9–10) and *Management Learning* (2012, Volume 43, Issue 3). In particular, the *British Journal of Management* has published influential works on the nature of management research (Tranfield and Starkey, 1998) and the double hurdles facing management researchers seeking to produce work that is both rigorous and relevant (Pettigrew, 1997; 2001). These special issues have opened up ways that management research, largely though not exclusively conducted in business schools, may inform the practice of those in managerial roles.

Journals play a more important role in management schools than professional domains such as engineering and medicine with which it is often compared and also foster applied research. Schools of medicine and engineering tend to be populated by those professionally trained in those areas. By contrast, management research is a messy, multidisciplinary meeting place characterised by porous boundaries and populated by researchers trained in a number of root disciplines including engineering, science, economics, sociology, psychology, history, social anthropology, etc. Indeed, it is sometimes claimed that there are more historians and sociologists in business schools than there are in history or sociology departments such is the relative popularity of business as a subject.

Whilst Pfeffer and Fong view this multidisciplinary melting pot as a source of paradigmatic weakness (2002) which inhibits the progress of management research, we advocate viewing this diversity as a source of strength in an increasingly multidisciplinary world. Pettigrew's observation that there "seems to be no natural focused community for our management research" (2011: 349) is consistent with the overall diversity of the field and its constituencies. However, this is only a problem if one regards management as a single discipline. An alternative view is that management is a field within which a range of disciplines co-exists, often with limited connection between them. Part of the academic challenge, as with the practical challenge, is connecting the sub-disciplines and developing an effective translation between their language games (e.g. connecting accounting with organisational behaviour (Beech and Anseel, 2020)). This need for cross-silo connectivity does, of course, make discussions of impact more complicated.

Aguinis et al. (2014) offer a pluralist conceptualisation of scholarly impact, identifying multiple potential stakeholders including students at various levels, corporate employees, unions, government policymakers, funding agencies, non-governmental organisations, accreditation organisations and the media.

Critical skills for impact

Having defined impact in a way which foregrounds collaboration, we suggest three ideas that might underpin impactful work: dialogue, praxis and reflexivity. Dialogue is not merely communication or an exchange of ideas. Rather, it is a process in which all participants are open to the possibility of being changed by the other, sometimes in uncomfortable or indeed discomforting ways (MacIntosh et al., 2012). Dialogue may represent one of the methods by which one set of ideas come into contact with another and is central to the collaborative exchanges that enable impact as defined here. There can be positive phases of co-production, but equally there can be disagreement and ideas that do not work as expected (Beech, 2008). In the transition from theory to practice, and back again, effective dialogue is crucial, enabling a relationship to persist over time during periods of "highs and lows".

Praxis is understood differently in various parts of the literature. Here, we argue that it is the pursuit of knowledge-infused practice, undertaken purposefully with the intention of fostering change. For all of those involved in the scholarly practice of impactful work, bringing about change in a situation is important. But so too is a change in our understanding of that situation. Understood in this way, praxis fosters impact across both the researcher and the researched.

Lastly, reflexivity is the process of critical self-questioning which facilitates the production of the self as the impactful research instrument. Theoretical knowledge is honed in traditional ways but, equally, it is honed through the struggle of trying to put it to use. Working in teams with diverse others leads to developing other languages and an elaboration of the self. Critically engaging with self-knowledge to recognise boundaries and limitations and move beyond them enables new ways of thinking and acting. And this requires people to be able to be vulnerable with each other – to express a *lack* of knowledge, to act with *uncertainty* and to *risk reputation* and the self. Hence, meta impact can give rise not only to changes in research practice that are enacted in future settings but also in changes to our story of ourselves as researchers. These reflexive and recursive (Hibbert et al., 2010) tendencies mean that as researchers we both shape, and are shaped by, the formative experience of journeying into the unknown. Underpinning dialogue, praxis and reflexivity, there needs to be an ethic of engagement, which provides a psychologically safe zone for such risky behaviour (Sealy et al., 2017). Although this can be difficult to achieve, and may take many years, it is what enables us to move into the unknown – which is the basis of research, learning and innovative practice.

When considered from the perspective of an individual researcher over an extended period, this moving into the unknown can have multiple consequences. A common objective in management research is to see new ideas adopted in the practice of organisational members, and most particularly amongst managers. Concluding peer-reviewed papers with a section on implications for practice is one move in this direction, and Bartunek and Rynes (2010) offer advice on the construction of such implications for practice and it is not uncommon for editorial policies to mandate or encourage their inclusion. Yet these well-intentioned attempts to translate from theory to practical implications tend to address the immediate rather than the meta, and, normally, they do not entail an empirical engagement over time to investigate how the practical implications work out in practice or how these "workings out" in turn influence the generation of new theory.

The focus on dialogue, reflexivity and praxis offers an opportunity to think more deeply about who is being impacted and in what ways. Expanding that thought process to include ourselves holds open the possibility of us, the researchers, being shaped by the very research that we conduct and the engagement that is part of impactful work.

On temporality and performativity

Working both with and beyond the immediacy of impact is challenging. Temporal insights are important and under explored in relation to engaged scholarship (e.g. Bartunek and Woodman, 2015; Albert and Bartunek, 2017). Particularly, when defined here, impact evolves over time as different participants make their own contributions, at different points in time. This, in turn, emphasises the importance of sequence. We note that just as impact evolves in longitudinal research settings, research questions can also evolve (MacIntosh et al., 2016) in ways that might influence both impact and those being impacted.

Albert and Bartunek (2017) suggest that in such collaborative, engaged situations, several temporal dimensions may be present in addition to sequence (the orders in which events occur). These include punctuation, interval, rate and polyphony. What is the punctuation of contributions? Do they happen only sporadically or continuously? At what intervals do they occur? Immediately? Long after a group starts? How quickly? Do contributions occur quickly after each other or after long periods of time? Does polyphony characterise them? For example, do academics and practitioners proceed across different tracks that nevertheless intersect with each other in productive ways (Bartunek, 2016)?

A key element of our conceptualisation of impact is that it is through theorising and practice that positive changes are imagined and made. This relationship is encapsulated in the concept of performativity. Performativity is concerned with the extent to which concepts, ideas and theories produce rather than simply describe the world and for academics, these means understanding what our theories do when they are used in practice. Mason et al. (2015) argue that theories in use shape practice in ways that both confirm some aspects of knowledge and reshape others. Theories, precisely because they are abstract and general, are always and necessarily transformed through practice (Barnes, 1983; MacKenzie, 2007: 56). As theories are picked up and put to work by practicing managers, not only do they help to produce the world by generating impact but they are also changed by it (Callon, 1998). This understanding is elaborated in Chapter 3 and also connects to our discussion of dialogue and co-influencing of collaborating actors in Chapter 4.

The impact map (see Figure 1.2) teases apart the form of impact being made and the group(s) being impacted. Though simplified, and though the identity categories used will likely exhibit some porosity and hybridity, it offers a way of thinking through our central question. Who is being impacted, in which way(s) and how does that change over time?

One form of impact is that of citation, largely where academics influence the work of other academics as theoretical developments, which typically appear in peer-reviewed publications shape future work. The more frequently a paper, idea or concept is cited in other peer-reviewed papers, the more impactful it is seen to have been. Time lags in this process of writing, then citing may partially explain why some practitioners believe the academic community to be "two or three cycles behind" (Beech et al., 2010: 1347). Further, we have already noted that citation is the dominant measure of impact within the academic community despite recognising that citation can be heightened by people avowedly disagreeing with the views espoused in a heavily cited paper. Nevertheless, we readily evaluate the merits of both individuals and ideas on the basis of h-indices and other similar citation measures (Bastow et al., 2014). It is also the case citation patterns are at least in part, performative. Some forms of outputs (e.g. review papers), in some particular outlets (e.g. typically prestigious journals), tend to receive higher citation precisely because we ascribe them higher status to begin with.

A second possibility is that the relation of theory to practice is such that the actions of practicing managers are based on theoretical knowledge that mostly comes directly or indirectly out of business and management schools (Sandelands, 1990; Czarniawska, 1999). There are high profile examples of models and frameworks impacting policy or practice to the extent that phrases like cash-cow and balanced score card become part of the managerial lexicon.

A third possibility is that ideas or concepts become embedded in the curricula of educational programmes in further or higher education, in the professions or both. Again, time lags can be at play meaning that new ideas can take time to become mainstream and that established ideas can take time to dislodge even where they have limited currency or relevance.

We often overlook the scale of the impact that management research has through education and learning. Our business schools teach students at a scale rarely seen in other disciplines and these individuals go on to inhabit managerial roles in a range of organisational settings. The impact of research on the curricula to which we teach generates a different form of citation where students legitimate their own thinking and acting with recourse to concepts, values and modes of inquiry which they have absorbed in classroom settings. Further, those professions that are allied to management (e.g. accountancy) absorb research and reify it in the form of accreditation standards whereby the status and practice of professionals become imbued with particular concepts, practices and frameworks.

Finally, impact may take the form of setting a research agenda within a particular field or prescribing the adoption of particular methodologies to further explore a phenomenon. Notably, a significant proportion of all published research concludes with suggestions for further research. This trope is also visible in calls that direct the attention of an entire sub-field such as the practice turn, the search for microfoundations in strategy and elsewhere, the rise (and fall) of Mode 2 knowledge production or the invocation to expand our use of methods that work with data sourced from ethnography to big data. Whilst such calls can also generate impact as citations, funding calls, opportunities, presidential addresses to learned societies, editorials and other communicative acts tend not to be cited straightforwardly in future research.

The impact map is not exhaustive but it does encourage a broader conceptualisation of impact. Indeed, we suggest that the four categories of impact that it sets out interact with each other over time. Indeed, their performativity may mean that one form of impact generates others. There are likely to be time lags and feedback loops at play which make it difficult to give a singular and definitive answer to the question with which we opened, that is, how, when and for whom does management research create impact? Rather, a processual, emergent and temporal perspective is required to see the overlaps, interplays and generative mechanisms that produce impact(s) (cf. Mason et al., 2015, 2019; Palo et al., 2020). This view of impact as a territory that can be inhabited in multiple ways suggests that we, as management researchers, need to consider how much we see ourselves engaged in a process of producing better artefacts (e.g. a new framework or model), producing better questions that shape an agenda, bettering our individual career or shaping the educational process by which future managers are prepared for their role(s). As Lambert and Enz note, rather than being rewarded for the number of "A" journal articles written, faculty members [could] be rewarded for the impact of their research on practice and the extent to which the research can be integrated into degree programme curricula and executive education programmes (2015: 13).

On the message and the medium

The real challenge, with this broader conceptualisation of impact, has been to understand the platforms, structures and praxis that might enable us as academics to engage and generate impact. Traditionally, print was the dominant dissemination channel with editorial control exerted either through peer review for academic outlets or through other structures for trade and mass media. In recent years, digital channels have fundamentally changed the process of dissemination across social media, professional networking sites and direct publishing in written, audio and video formats. The pace and plurality of dissemination continue to change. Some have referred to the use of these various platforms, structures and practices as pathways to impact. Our experience and review of the evidence are that there is no simple, linear pathway to impact. In fact, the very notion of a pathway can imply an ordering of practices from research through translation to implementation. Here, we first identify some of those pathways before considering the temporal implications such pathways have for engagements and their performativities.

Platforms are the social-material structures upon which academics can stand with the explicit purpose of reaching other stakeholders. They include university and learned society websites designed to translate scholarly research for practice across many scholarly areas and enable engagement and impact. These sources often provide "digests" and succinct papers which disseminate research findings in a way that is designed to be accessible. Generally, these would be Type Two impact. Four examples are Behavioral Scientist, Impact Science, the Entrepreneur and Innovation Exchange and The Conversation. Scholarly associations often sponsor their own practitioner-facing platforms. Two examples are the international association of Chinese management research magazine called Management Insights and the Academy of Management's AOM Insights. In addition, professional bodies sponsor, produce and reproduce research to publish practice reports. For example, the Chartered Institute of Personnel and Development both run a conference that combines papers and practical workshops and it publishes frameworks, practice guidance and examples. Similarly, the Chartered Management Institute publishes best practice advice and reports drawn from expert practitioner input. These activities would be types two and four impacts. Lastly, publishers, in addition to publishing practitioner-oriented magazines and journals, also publish books written by both academics and professionals aimed at practitioners.

These platforms, as ways of reaching other stakeholders, primarily through dissemination are given in Table 1.1. The table sets out alternative platforms and for each specifies who leads on the production of the

Table 1.1 Platforms for reaching other stakeholders

Lead	Content	Impact type	Characterised by
University websites and publications	Succinct papers	2	Dissemination and promoting the university
Learned societies	Repots and applied research papers	2,4	Dissemination and serving members
Professional bodies	Practice reports	2,4	Serving members by picking up novelty
Publisher	Practitioner journals	2	Academics writing for practitioner audiences
	Books	2,4	Academics writing for practitioners
			Practitioner writing for practitioners

platform, its content, the types of impact achievable (using the types in the impact map) and examples that characterise the way the platform is put into action.

Structures are taken here to refer to the socio-material arrangement of relations between multiple stakeholders and other complex elements. In contrast to platforms (that are understood as a particular form of structure upon which academics can stand to disseminate insights to practitioners), more generally, structures provide places and spaces of engagement, dialogue, praxis and reflexivity, fostering multi-stakeholder communities purposed with generating change and impact. One of the most traditional places where this happens might teaching spaces, particularly, in executive education and continuous professional development, business schools undertake the impact of Type Two. Type Four impact can be seen in the consulting activities of universities in companies and in the industry clubs, benchmarking networks and associations that many business schools run, often with either an industry focus (such as banking, retail, manufacturing or public sector) or a thematic focus (such as environmental sustainability or innovation), see Table 1.2 for a summary.

Other actors also provide interactive structures. For example, Learned Societies provide web resources and workshops, as do professional bodies,

Table 1.2 Structures for interacting with stakeholders

Lead	Content	Impact type	Characterised by
Universities	Industry clubs and associations	4	Focused networks, typically operating over time
	Executive education and CPD	2	Company-specific or generic training on research-focused topics
	Teaching	1,2	Dissemination plus engagement and potentially action
	Consulting	4	Use of research knowledge on specific company problems
Learned societies	Interactive web resources and workshops	2,4	Interaction on focal topics Translation and engagement
Professional bodies	Interactive web resources and workshops	2,4	Interaction on focal topics Translation and engagement
Consultancies	Practitioner journals books	2,4	Promoting particular topics Translating research

and these can be Types Two or Four impact. Consultancies also operate such structures, developing toolkits, workshops, media dissemination and direct advice, again being Types Two and Four impact.

For each of these structures, it is the dialogic, praxis and reflexivity that are held together and performed by these structures, which unfold what kinds of impacts are achieved, with whom and how.

We have defined *praxis* as the pursuit of knowledge-infused practice, undertaken purposefully with the intention of fostering change. Within these structures, the relational praxis between scholars, practicing managers and policymakers is foreground. In contrast with the platform examples, where research is carried out and the insights are translated, made accessible and circulated in different ways to different audiences and stakeholders, the structures described here are more typically held together by praxis that are far less linear in their pathway of research to impact. Researching–impacting can be concurrent, complex, disparate and entangled with the co-production of insight. In each case, it is the structured relational praxis between scholars, practicing managers and policymakers that determines performance; what can be performed, by whom, with what effect.

Relationships between academics and practitioners have been present within the social sciences for many years. These started, most probably, with action research (Lewin, 1947) and organisation development (Bartunek and Moch, 1987), extending through forms of shared research such as insider/outsider team research (Bartunek and Louis, 1996), Mode 2 (Tranfield and Starkey, 1998) and engaged scholarship (Van de Ven, 2007).

Bartunek (2007) discussed the need for what she called "a relational scholarship of integration", including forums for joint academic/practitioner discussion. Romme et al. (2015) discussed the value of "trading zones" between academics and practitioners, forums that would enable collaboration and engagement between academic and practitioner communities. Many of the papers published in the special issue on Impact published in the *British Journal of Management* focused on long-term relationships between academics and practitioners. A discussion of the wide range of forms of academic-practitioner relationships was published by Bartunek and McKenzie (2018). These include, among others, ways that academics and practitioners might collaborate to design indicators of global values (Landman et al., 2018) and how businesses such as google may benefit from academic involvement (Kurkoski, 2018). In addition, Carton and Dameron (2018) indicated how academic-practitioner collaboration has led to the development of and popularisation of a number of constructs, such as blue ocean strategy and business model canvas. In other words, there are a wide range of ways that academics and practitioners can collaborate successfully.

It is useful to reflect here on the way that alternative engagement praxis is constituted from bundles of practice performed by participants. As Van de Ven (2007) and others point out, collaboration is a "team sport" in which different skills and know-how are brought to bear in crafting a process and outcomes and this relies on relationships that are sufficiently trusting to enable learning, errors, changing minds and exciting discoveries. Over time, the roles and relationships can change and typically have an influence on each other. In part, this is because the boundaries of know-how become blurred as people learn skills from each other. Significantly, however, as a collaboration lasts over time, the participants become changed through their involvement – they begin to see the context and the practices from the perspective of the collaborative venture rather than their original starting point. We are not suggesting that all impact is like this, it remains the case that instrumental and contractual exchange can effectively bring about change in organisations, but in long-lasting impactful work, the relationships, processes and practices are all likely to be modified because of the engagement.

When viewed from multiple audiences or stakeholder perspectives, impact pathways, if they do exist, have different appearances and orderings. What has begun illustrated here is that the starting point could be a recognition of an issue in practice and a commissioning of research to solve the problem. Alternatively, there may be no distinct separation of research, experimentation and developmental practice. Researchers, managers, practitioners, commissioners and funders may play a variety of roles and have alternative interpretations of what is really going on and why.

The end of the beginning

We believe that management research can and should matter. It matters differently to different audiences, in different ways and at different times. In that sense, our central argument in this book is that impactful management research is a complex process that demands a reframing of who is involved, the skills that are needed and an approach that is both nuanced and action-oriented – in short, what is needed is practical knowledge of how to produce practical knowledge. This book is intended to contribute to the understanding of such practical knowledge.

We acknowledge the different and potentially diffuse audiences for whom impact may, or may not, occur. Through an exposition of impact over time, we problematise traditional notions of sequence, such as upstream/downstream and theory/practice. Within a co-constituted impact landscape, where "the practices constituting a legitimate enactment of a popular concept varies over time, between and even within organizations, it remains unclear which iteration represents the concept" (Wilhelm and Bort, 2013: 430). Thus, impact is accounted for differently by different communities on different bases. In recognising this, we suggest that there are implications for the management research community, not least in the ways in which we induct and train new members of our community.

Management research has long-drawn lessons from other disciplines, notably medicine and engineering (see Tranfield and Starkey, 1998). In previous decades, our discipline aspired to the "idea of an 'administrative science' that would apply the insights of social science to the problem of managing bureaucracies just as engineering applies the insights of natural science to design" (Davis, 2015: 179). However, there are dangers in such aspirations if they are taken to imply another version of "upstream–downstream" orientation which also characterises the distinction between "pure" and "applied" research. These dangers include marginalising research that is grounded, inductively oriented or practice-based. Many research traditions start with experiences in the field and develop more general insight and theory from there. For example, sociology or social anthropology of work may be no more or less pure or applied than similarly oriented management research. Much of the scholarship in such fields argues against hierarchical distinctions, which might inhibit the very dialogic orientation that the papers in our special issue highlight as central to impact. Whilst we might learn from medicine and engineering, we might equally learn from a range of other disciplines. Some which may be of particular interest are those that have performance or practice at their heart, such as literature, music, drama and art (Creech, 2008). For example, Adler (2015) showed how art can inspire leaders, and Styhre (2016) and Patriotta (2016) have shown what management scholars can learn from great literature.

Similarly, the formative training process in fields such as education and nursing interweaves the lecture theatre with periods of observed practice and reflection in schools and hospitals, often following Schön's (1983) model of reflective practice. These disciplines bring academic analysis to practice to work with practitioners such that performance becomes influenced by new thinking and theory can become embodied in performance (Gabor, 2013). Equally, theory picks up insight from practice. This may involve some co-production with academics and practitioners/performers together or may be undertaken over time with some meetings and working together and some work apart, and this would appear to be closer to the examples in the papers in this Special Issue than a traditional notion of "pure" and "applied" work.

We are struck by the fact that few business or management academics observe their students practising management in organisational settings before offering them critical feedback. Further, we are struck by the different language, tone and conclusions that a book on impactful management research might feature were it to be written by those who foreground "manager" in their identity narrative rather than "academic".

We must pay particular attention to how management and organisation research is purposefully picked up and put to work in daily working lives. This requires a more nuanced understanding of how managers and policymakers come to encounter and engage with research findings and theories, and how they and other key actors transform those theories through their use: in practice (cf. MacKenzie, 2006). We have already suggested ways of mapping the network configurations and devices (i.e. mapping who we work with, where and how, what theories we invoke and transform, for what practical purpose), assembled to support impact occurring for specific constituents. This is more than the simplistic sense of setting out pathways to impact in a research grant application and we encourage greater emphasis on impact being *designed in* to a process of inquiry which will itself evolve over time.

This deceptively simple reversal of logic could be transformative to research practices themselves suggesting new forms of collaborative working between academics and outside constituents. Equally, we would acknowledge that anti-performativity, that is, a deep-seated aversion towards any type of theorising which may directly or serendipitously find some practical implications in the hands of managers, is an important touchstone for those within our community engaged in critical management studies (Fournier and Grey, 2000).

A crucial part of understanding who is involved is to be aware of the way those agents are prepared for, and come to, collaborative processes. There is frequently a focus in academia on "early career researchers" and doctoral training, which includes technical training and cultural assimilation into the norms of the community. In most social groupings, status and hierarchy play an important structuring role and this is no less true in academia where we have criteria and measures for discerning status differentials. Part of the socialisation of early career people is their internalisation, and enactment, of status. As our academic culture is particularly concerned with objectivity, evidence and logic, the performativity of "being a good academic" becomes adorned with this discourse. So there is a focus on research grants from the *right* sources, publications in the *leading* journals and citation metrics. Whilst there is certainly value in objectivity, evidence and logic, there is also evidence that some of the metrics we use as vicarious measures may not support the meritocratic hierarchy that is supposed to exist in universities. For example, citations and seniority of position in universities, professional bodies and learned societies may reflect both ability and privilege. To take a relatively simple example, gender, ethnicity, disability and age, for example, may impact on the potential for informal networking which influences positions such as editorships, which in turn influences the level of recognition and influence ("citability") that person has in their sub-field. So the academic meritocracy may be a social construct that relies on the quality of work plus other factors. Our proposal is that early career academics should be trained and socialised to understand Type One impact – where the academic community impacts upon itself – but should understand this with critical reflexivity. That is, they should have the opportunity to understand the performativity of this type of work and to be able to question it through the use of well-founded evidence and logic. In addition, it is important that early career academics should understand the possibilities of other forms of impact and that these should be part of academic training and socialisation. Clearly, a barrier to this is the status associated with different types of achievement, and so it is also important that we challenge the systems of appointment and promotion to ensure that they are based on a sound understanding of equality, diversity and inclusion as they relate to the performativity of an academic career and the value of different types of impact.

In addition to developing broader skills in early career academics, there should be an equal focus on mid-career academics and professionals/ practitioners. If we believe that much impactful work entails inter-disciplinarity and trans-disciplinarity, and that this is a "team sport", academics need a sufficient foundation in their discipline to contribute to the collaborative outcome. Academics who are experienced in their own discipline can bring a depth of knowledge to project teams, but to be successful they may benefit from developing skills in collaborative working and a sufficient insight into other disciplines and practices. In Chapter 6, we discuss a career-long framework for academic development which has been developed by the British Academy of Management. Lastly, we should be considering how professional practitioners may be enabled to take fully active roles in project teams. This may be achieved through them having time and responsibility allocated to the project within their workplace, but equally it can include secondments, practitioner fellowships or professional-in-residence schemes in business schools which enable time and space for dialogue and reflexivity which may not be achieved in the same way whilst in the day-to-day activities of the workplace.

Initial proposals for understanding how, when and for whom management research creates impact

Our search for impact is unnecessarily inhibited and narrow if the locus of our explorations is restricted exclusively to the pages of peer-reviewed journals. Our classrooms, our curricula and our relationships to the professions and to practice each matter at least as much. In the remainder of this book, we set out further details on the contexts and timing of impact (Chapter 2), impact as theory in use (Chapter 3), dialogue as an enabler of impact (Chapter 4), ethical considerations in impact (Chapter 5) before drawing these insights together in a framework for impactful management research (Chapter 6). Given the importance of the topic, and with a sense of irony and trepidation, we hope that in so doing we are making an impact of sorts, and our initial proposals at this stage of the journey are as follows:

1   Impact should be understood not as an event but as a process over time which grows through dialogue, reflexivity and praxis.
2   We define impact as evidenced change occurring as a result of the purposeful application of co-developed knowledge.
3   The participants should be reframed as agents within complex (social and technical) systems which develop and apply practical knowledge. Academic practitioners and professional practitioners bring different, complementary skills to the collaboration, and each needs to be given their appropriate role in the process.
4   There are different types of impact which relate to particular audiences and purposes. These types also relate to modes of connecting between actors in "platforms" and "structures".
5   Impact occurs at immediate and meta levels and delivers different types of value. Therefore, it is important to design, fund and evaluate projects in a way that encapsulates all of the value produced, not a small subset of value.
6   Impactful work is typically interdisciplinary and entails working on non-discrete problems and opportunities which do not fit neatly into academic or organisational silos. Therefore, there is a need for training that enables effective action in the intersection between disciplines and practices.

2 Delivering impact in management research

How relationships foster impactful outcomes

Contexts and timing in impact

To begin our exploration of impact in management research, it is important to note that the academy is changing. In days now past, universities appeared largely insulated from the vagaries of policy and the pressures of economic performance. Those working in modern university contexts can glimpse fragments of those halcyon days at retirement functions or through accounts from Emeritus colleagues of how things used to be. Many of the most commonly used management ideas were generated by academics conducting research with the deliberate intention to help managers to manage more effectively. Yet, at the point at which those ideas were produced, there was less overt management of our management research. There was also less overt attention paid to the kind of purposeful co-development of knowledge that characterises impact.

Newly qualified members of today's academy, particularly in our schools of business and management, face expectations with sharper edges than those of their predecessors. The pressure to perform, both individually and institutionally, is omnipresent, moulding the very act of research itself. When choosing topics to pursue, there is a focus on where funding might be found. When applying for those research funds, there is an expectation that pathways to impact will be clear. Having conducted research, the journey to publication focuses ruthlessly on novelty because claims to contribution frame the editorial processes which determine those papers that will appear in the most prestigious outlets. Those outlets themselves are subject to their own, nested performance pressures in the form of rankings, lists and citation data.

Whilst caricaturing for effect, it is possible to romanticise a bygone era where ideas mattered for their own sake, where impact sometimes happened and sometimes didn't and where individual careers were given time to blossom. Making the transition from a doctoral programme to a junior academic position requires that individuals account for their performance relative to expectations and metrics which seem ever more demanding. In this chapter, we will explore the ways in which relationships shape impact. In Chapter 1, we argued that impact is best understood as a process of purposeful co-development, and now we will begin to consider the outlook of academic researchers and of other actors.

We will begin with a brief reflection on the status of management as topic for academic research and the funding landscape in which that research is conducted. We then move on to consider the contextual factors influencing research and the temporal dimensions of impact in management research before concluding with recommendations on the design, execution and dissemination of impactful research.

Management as a profession

Management itself is a broad term and our schools of business and management offer homes to scholars from a variety of backgrounds of other disciplines including psychology, economics, sociology, anthropology and engineering. Our curricula and our research tend to map into reasonably well-defined groupings such as marketing, human resource management and logistics. There are large learned societies that focus on general management which may feature divisions or special interest groups with narrower scope. There are also specialist learned societies dedicated to the pursuit of knowledge in particular sub-disciplines. Both the general and the specialist learned societies hold conferences and publish journals to disseminate new ideas.

For illustrative purposes, let's contrast strategic management and accountancy. Those who specialise in strategy as a discipline believe that strategy matters above all else in organisational terms. As a group of four authors, we have differing subject specialisms and the zealous belief that strategy matters most is not uniformly shared but, as educators, we do share a believe that studying something (e.g. strategy) can make your practice (e.g. as a strategist) more informed and perhaps more effective.

Strategy, however, is a subject with different schools of thought, different traditions and approaches, a variety of analytical models and roots into a range of other disciplines such as economics, sociology and systems theory. It is, therefore, hard to argue that strategy is a profession that requires formal adherence to a single, agreed curriculum because there is no unifying concept of strategy. No professional body acts as guardian or gatekeeper and, therefore, there is no way to stop someone from claiming to be a strategist. A cursory examination of key texts in strategy research reveals fundamentally differing world views on the ontological and epistemological status of strategy. Similar arguments could be made for marketing, human resource management and many other specialisms. Barker (2010) and many others have argued that management is not a profession for these reasons.

Following the financial crisis of 2007–2008, business schools were subject to criticism when alumni of high profile schools oversaw the collapse of major financial institutions. Enron generated one form of scandal and sub-prime mortgages another. Khurana and Nohria (2008) argued that it was time to make management a profession, even going as far as to draft a Hippocratic oath.

In contrast to either the specific sub-discipline of strategy, or indeed the case for general management as a whole, accountancy is widely accepted as a profession. Multiple professional associations, in multiple geographies, oversee both university curricula and post-university, professional qualifications. To attain the status of a professional accountant, individuals must study prescribed topics, demonstrate competence at prescribed tasks and comply with agreed definitions. Whilst particular sub-domains of accounting research might problematise emerging areas such as environmental accounting, core ideas such as profit, loss, assets and liability are defined, agreed and subject to audit. Whilst it is perfectly feasible to develop strategy absent any formal education or training in the subject, it is not feasible to declare oneself an accountant and lodge formal records of your organisation's financial performance. Disagreeing with the way in which someone has conducted a SWOT analysis is not a criminal offence. Misstating your organisation's financial position is.

Millerson (1964) classified professions as qualifying associations, occupational associations, prestige associations and study associations to denote the overlapping remits and priorities each pursues. This work to classify professions persists (e.g. Segon et al., 2019) yet, whilst a number of membership organisations have sprung up, no singular or unifying concept of management, or indeed management practice has emerged.

This lack of agreed norms is part problem, part opportunity particularly when new phenomena appear. The emergence of blockchain as a technology is a good example. Predicted to reshape the ways in which commercial relationships are formed, executed and monitored, it is not yet widely understood or adopted. Are there differences in which strategists and accountants might learn about then amend their practice in response to a new technology such as blockchain? The answer is yes, but it is less straightforward to know whether a strong professional identity, stable core concepts and accepted practices are good or bad in relation to a rapidly changing technological environment since it rather depends on one's viewpoint and intention.

The funding landscape

A second contextual consideration in producing impactful management research is the mechanism(s) of funding of that research. Research funding for any discipline is important in at least three ways in contemporary university settings. First, it enables research by buying time for the principal investigator and their team where others are involved too. Second, it is seen as an indicator of quality and often used in assessments or rankings which draw the attention of senior university managers, potential students, potential research partners and a range of other stakeholders. Third, it can and does influence individual career progression.

Applying a narrower focus by considering the funding of management research, each of these three views can be particularised. First, the idea of buying time for a principal investigators and their team sits comfortably in a science, technology, engineering or mathematics (STEM) setting where this mode of research is the norm. Bidding for monies to buy equipment, laboratory time, technician support and research assistance seems eminently sensible for experimental research but this model of research applies only to a subset of management research. The costs associated with experimental forms of STEM research tend to be high meaning that award amounts are larger. The attraction for national governments and other funders of breakthrough technologies also tends to mean that the STEM research receives a higher levels of funding. A recent census of research funding in the UK found that over the last ten years the STEM subjects received an average increase in total research funding of 63% compared to 11% for Business and Management. Adjusting for inflation over this period, this translates to an average increase of 21% for the STEM subjects and a fall of 18% for Business and Management (Chartered Association of Business Schools, 2020).

This connects to the second view of research funding as a proxy for quality which often features in institutional assessments and rankings. The UK has a particularly well-established practice of measuring research performance through what its Research Excellence Framework (REF) which is entering its sixth iteration.[1] REF 2014 incorporated impact alongside research outputs and research environment for the first time, with the REF 2021 exercise allocating 25% of the overall research assessment to impact which is defined as "an effect on, change or benefit to the economy, society, culture, public policy or services, health, the environment or quality of life, beyond academia" (REF 2021 Guidance on Submissions). Similar assessment frameworks exist in other countries but even where there is no national assessment of research performance, universities can be compared on the percentage of their income derived from research grants and this is a criteria used in rankings such as the Times Higher Education (THE) World University Rankings. Whilst noting that research income is a controversial indicator "because it can be influenced by national policy and economic circumstances", the THE note that "income is crucial to the development of world-class research, and because much of it is subject to competition and judged by peer review, our experts suggested that it was a valid measure". In exercises of this type, research income is modelled to reflect the disciplinary composition of each university's portfolio of subject since "research grants in science subjects are often bigger than those awarded for the highest-quality social science, arts and humanities research" as noted earlier. The relative scarcity of research funding for management research means that rankings of this type are problematic. We return to the performative conse-quences of research assessment regimes in Chapter 6.

The third lens through which funding for management research can be viewed is that of individual career progression. In a context where larger numbers of academic staff compete for relatively scarcer research funds, it is challenging for early career management researchers to flourish. Indeed, there is a further dilemma. Working closely with practice (e.g. industry, public or third sector partners) not only helps establish pathways to impact but also raises the expectation that these partner organisations should them-selves fund research directly. Beech and Anseel (2020) suggest that "man-agement research needs to further embrace a problem-driven approach and seek to add value to organizations, businesses and society by helping address pressing problems" but securing funding for such research can be difficult. To calibrate expectations of excellence, there are indications that a tiny minority of tenured professors at leading US schools of business and management hold research funding.[2]

Contextual factors

Having reviewed the nature of management as a discipline and the funding landscape in which research is conducted, we now turn to consider three nested contextual factors that influence the extent to which management research achieves impact. We will argue that individual, organisational and sectoral contexts influence impact both individually and collectively.

Individual researchers are individuals first and foremost. Some will be more inclined to conduct management research with the intention of gen-erating impact than others. There could be multiple reasons for such indi-vidual differences. We have already noted that management itself draws in ideas and scholars from different root disciplines such as anthropology, sociology, psychology, economics and engineering. Each of these root dis-ciplines will have norms about the relationship between theory and prac-tice. Tranfield and Starkey argued that schools of business and management could helpfully mimic the relationship between medical schools and medi-cal practice (1998). Management research, they suggest, should be a pro-cess where new scientific discoveries are converted into practices that have the explicit intention of helping managers understand what works, in what circumstances and why. Returning to an earlier theme from this chapter, one of the challenges with this analogy is that one scholar pursuing management as applied psychology may not be able to agree on the definition of terms with a colleague studying management as applied sociology. This is further exacerbated if there is no agreement on methods, reliability, etc. Susman and Evered note that "positivist science works with a view that knowledge can only be produced when data can directly be obtained, experienced, verified and repeated between independent observers" (1978: 583) yet much management research does not subscribe to a positivist mindset in framing the nature of research, new knowledge or evidence. Indeed, some management researchers would rail at the very notion of a singular, fixed reality amenable to the kinds of independently verifiable testing that Susman and Evered attribute to positivist science. In other traditions of research, there is a far greater emphasis on the particularities of given situations even to the extent that research questions themselves can "legitimately change over time during the conduct of field-based, longitudinal action research" (MacIntosh et al., 2016: 48).

Levels of interest in producing impact may vary from one individual researcher to another but even where there is a shared intention to aim for impact, disciplinary and/or epistemological differences may be at play. If individual academic researchers talk past each other because of such, often unspoken, differences, what hope is there when trying to communicate ideas to practicing managers? This challenge becomes even more pronounced if the intention is to engage practicing managers in the co-development of ideas that make a difference.

Where there is an intention to conduct research that impacts on practice, some argue that it is important to frame the research "in the context of application" (Gibbons et al., 1994). That is to say to start with a problem rather than to start with the theory. There are few better examples of theory-led research than the use of the Large Hedron Collider at CERN to confirm the existence of the so-called Higgs Boson. Peter Higgs had speculated on a theoretical possibility in 1964 but it took a huge investment to create the apparatus required to prove his theoretical insight. The joint award of the Nobel Prize to Higgs and François Englert in 2013 represented the culmination of a long, theory-led journey. Problem-led research starts with an articulation of a matter of "genuine concern" (Eden and Huxham, 1996) to those in the organisational setting(s) where the research will be conducted. This approach requires a dialogue with actors in those organisational settings (Beech et al., 2010). The imperative to be practically useful, rather than theoretically curious, should be the dominant consideration in framing new research projects where the starting point is that research is produced under "continuous negotiation" (Gibbons et al., 1994: 3) with practicing managers.

However, we must acknowledge that individual preference and purpose hold significance. For some, management is a phenomena to be studied at arm's length whilst for others it may be a process, perhaps even one which is co-constructed through social interaction. Harshly stylised, this could be presented as the difference between a tendency to conduct "research on management" or "research with managers". Shotter distinguished between what he called "thinking 'from within' and 'from the outside', or between 'withness'- and 'aboutness'-thinking" (2006: 586).

Given our definition of impact as a process of co-development, we argue that impact involves "withness" rather than "aboutness". However, regardless of whether individuals incline to forms of research that privilege practical relevance or approach the process of research with the prior intention of delivering impact, the organisational context in which the research is conducted also shapes outcomes.

Organisations vary just as individuals do. One of the ways in which we address this variation is to think about the norms, expectations and behaviours that seem acceptable in one setting yet less acceptable in another. Organisational culture is sometimes defined as "how we do things round here" (Drennan, 1992) and, despite the manifest differences in the ways in which organisational culture itself is theorised in the literature, at some more abstract level, it is possible to imagine different levels of value being placed on the role of management theory in different organisations.

For illustrative purposes, imagine two different organisations. The first was founded by an entrepreneur who left school with no formal qualifications and now leads a large, multi-divisional organisation that has a culture where action is what matters. The second was founded by a small group of MBA graduates who spotted a gap in an existing market during coursework conducted as part of their studies. The design of their business model, operating systems, incentive schemes and hiring practices were shaped by models and frameworks taught as received wisdom in the MBA classroom. The prevailing attitudes to management theory would likely vary within these two organisations, not least because the hiring practices would continually reinforce those attitudes.

In a previous study, we asked practicing managers their views of academics and of academic research (see Beech et al., 2010). The responses we received made clear the differing organisational contexts in which management research might take place:

> Who in their right mind would go to an academic for advice on how to run a business?
>
> (op cit. p1351)

> The academic community is two or three cycles behind practice. We are more use to them than they are to us.
>
> (op cit. p1349)

In a big organizational change experience, it [the presence of academic researchers] has allowed us to kind of, just pause and seek reassurance or ground what we're . . . That's been key for us. The learning and the reassurance that flows from that is important.

(op cit. p1347)

The appetite of individual management researchers to strive for impactful research, therefore, interacts with an audience of practicing managers who may or may not place value on academic ideas as a source of guidance. The three examples quoted earlier indicate a range of possible organisational settings from outright hostility, to guarded expectations of who might benefit from interactions to a more positive sense of reassurance that *your* management practice represents *good*, or indeed *best*, practice. Our contention here is that the receptiveness, or otherwise, of managers whose practice you may wish to impact, will vary partly as a result of personal preference and partly as a consequence of the prevailing organisational culture in which that practice takes place. This is entirely consistent with the relational and processual view of impact which we are advocating and suggests that a narrower, theory-first chronology unnecessarily restricts our ability to explain, let alone achieve impact.

And that is not all. A third contextual factor is that of industry maturity. Manufacturing businesses began to take recognisable form during the industrial revolution of the late 18th century. As the so-called mass production emerged, so too did ways of managing production to maximise efficiency. Work-study, layout planning, inventory management and production planning techniques developed because there were sufficient similarities in the manufacturing of different products to allow the same techniques to apply. Therefore, if you are researching productivity in manufacturing settings, methodologies like Lean Six Sigma draw on reasonably well-developed knowledge, frameworks, training and expertise. Industry maturity generates a stability that affords both management researchers and practicing managers the opportunity for dialogue about what works in which circumstances and why.

In contrast, new business models in emerging new industries are, by their very nature, contested and not well understood. When the idea for a business that would become Twitter evolved in 2006, no one knew how the underpinning business model would work. A social media revolution had started but not yet become the omnipresent force which it is today. Twitter seemed an unusual proposition. We now know that the ability to follow someone without the need for this to be reciprocated played to a fixation with celebrity and crowd-sourced news/fake news but messages which, at launch, were limited to 140 characters seemed unlikely to catch on. Ev Williams, Twitter's CEO, was clear about being unclear claiming that "rather than attach advertising to a personal communication channel, we want to make it a benefit . . . we think those things have potential, so as the userbase grows we'll flesh out which of those things work and the business model and revenue will fit in". Conducting management research in an industry which is being formed in real time is a very different proposition to management research in an industry with well-defined processes, models, structures, etc. Perhaps 3D printing will radically alter our understanding of supply chains in manufacturing settings. Earlier, we mentioned blockchain as another potentially disruptive technology and, of course, our universities are subject to a wave of online innovation as a result of the global coronavirus pandemic. Mature industries do, however, offer more stable settings in which refinement and adaption of existing ideas might occur.

Tying individual, organisational and industry levels together, it is possible to unpack one part of our overarching question: where does management research have impact? Individual researchers motivated to generate impact may conduct their studies in organisational contexts that are receptive to and place value on academic research, and those organisational contexts may be in industries that are mature enough to have established management practices that are amenable to study, refine and improve. Of course, the opposite could also be true. Researchers may not be trying to generate impact but could do so inadvertently. Organisations may not place value on the idea of academic research but may, perhaps because of this, be disruptive, innovative spaces where new management practices emerge. Finally, a rapidly changing industry influenced by regulatory forces, technological breakthroughs or both may *lead* management research or be shaped by it. We, therefore, next turn our attention to issues of timing.

Temporality and impact

Research grant applications are not unlike business plans in that both make predictions about what will happen in the future absent any concrete knowledge of that future. We produce a justification for the research which sets out which questions we will ask and how these will build on existing knowledge. We then set out a plan to address those questions covering issues such as data gathering, analysis and ethics. We may even set out our plans for dissemination and how we plan to achieve impact from our work. All of this will be chronologically ordered to produce a sense of reassurance to the funder that the research is both worthwhile and feasible. However, these promissory notes are guesses about what might happen. The reality can be quite different.

In Chapter 1, we set developed an impact map (see Figure 1.2) as a means of exploring why our intention to transition smoothly from research to impact is beyond our direct control. We now return to four types of impact set out in Chapter 1.

For academics seeking to impact the thinking of other academics (Type One), a practical impediment is the time and risk associated with peer-reviewed publication. Clearly, findings could be disseminated through other channels instantly but the prestige of appearing in a highly cited journal is a powerful draw relative to a self-published blog. Peer review takes time and runs the risk that the paper itself is rejected. Open access introduces new challenges for researchers and citation patterns can be influenced by other activities such as conferences, workshops and seminars to help draw attention to research that might otherwise sink without trace amidst a sea of other similar studies.

A related, but separate, second context for impact (Type Two) is to share future research agendas or to propose new methods to study existing phenomena. Again, achieving impact in this way is dependent upon an ability to reach and influence your audience. Perhaps it is not an accident that most of the research papers conclude with advice on areas for further study and reflections on the limitations of the methods employed to date.

Where there is a concern to influence management practice by bringing forward new ideas in the form of frameworks or models dissemination changes slightly. It is still possible that peer-reviewed publication will reach an audience of practicing managers but, more likely, other intermediary platforms such as books, podcasts or trade-press articles will act to translate findings and advice into digestible form (Type Three). Finally, reaching practicing managers indirectly by shaping the curricula of taught programmes and/or the expectations for professional or accrediting bodies (Type Four) represents a powerful way of enforcing reach.

Two further points highlight the temporal dimensions of these pathways to different types of impact. First, consider speed at which ideas are taken up by fellow researchers. In strategy research, one of the most heavily used ideas of recent years has been that of dynamic capability, that is, the capacity of a firm to change the way it operates over time. Contemporary literature sources point to two seminal papers by Teece et al. (1997) and by Eisenhardt and Martin (2000) both of which have been heavily cited. However, the roots of dynamic capabilities can be traced further back to the work of Edith Penrose and her book *The Theory of the Growth of the Firm* published in 1959. This important work sought to examine the ways in which firms developed specific resources which helped them to engage with their external environment but it lays largely dormant in the literature until Birger Wernerfelt published the Resource-Based View of the Firm in 1984 signalling a desire to pay more attention to this more inward looking take on competitiveness. Further elaboration of these ideas occurred when Jay Barney published a paper suggesting that firms can build competitive advantage if they nurture resources which are valuable, rare and difficult to imitate (1991). In the case of dynamic capabilities, impact has slowly gathered momentum over decades.

Second, consider the possibility of failure. Tourish argues that "really worthwhile work takes time, autonomy and the freedom to fail, often" (2019: 79). He goes on to suggest that research grants should only be awarded to those who can demonstrate and that research funding should only go to those who can demonstrate that some of their prior research failed since this indicates a capacity to tackle big questions with uncertain answers. Whilst he is no doubt being provocative to evoke a response, there is an underlying truth that research where the answers are already known is both easier to write into a funding bid yet also not really research at all.

In striving for impact it is important to recognise that it may be achieved slowly, accidentally even, and not always as intended.

Conclusions

In this chapter, we have explored the context(s) in which impact might occur. We have considered nature of management itself and established that, whilst sub-disciplines such as accountancy are recognised as a profession, general management is not. We have reviewed the challenges of funding management research as compared to STEM subjects and we have set out the individual, organisational and sectoral perspectives that might shape impactful research. Finally, we have noted that impact itself may occur slowly, organically over time even following periods where it might appear that no impact has occurred. Ideas have their time and influential ideas can ebb and flow into (and back out of) fashion.

What then does this tell us about impactful management research? How should one approach the challenge of designing, executing and disseminating management research to achieve impact? We would recommend thinking about people, place and profession as a useful way of maximising the likelihood of impact.

First, think about the people that you are hoping to impact with your research. Are you trying to impact on the work of fellow academic researchers, practicing managers or both? Researchers and practicing managers operate in different environments and will likely be swayed by different communication strategies and this should shape your approach to dissemination. More provocatively, dissemination itself privileges the idea of academics having valuable knowledge which they willingly pass on to practicing managers who don't possess that knowledge. Approaching impact from the perspective of a two-way dialogue, as discussed in Chapter 4, may yield a richer dynamic.

Second, think about places. Alongside peer-reviewed publications, there are other places that management ideas might gain traction. Indeed peer-reviewed publication, even in open-access outlets and even where the journal concerned is prestigious, may have very limited reach even within academia. How many practicing managers do you know who maintain subscriptions to peer-reviewed journals? And amongst this small group, how many read the contents regularly with the intention of changing their management practice? Blogs, podcasts and TED talks are far more likely to reach practicing managers but little if no attention is paid to these platforms. They are modern supplements to books or trade-press articles where the communicative form can be less restricted and more direct absent the pressure to locate your new ideas in the extant literature to the satisfaction of peer reviewers. We return to the idea of platforms in Chapter 6 and reflect in more detail on the skills required to communicate effectively in these new ways.

Classrooms and curricula likewise represent a powerful means of influencing practice but are places which are perhaps undervalued. Classrooms are, however, populated by a subset of practicing (or at least aspiring future) managers who have demonstrated a predisposition to learning about management. Using this captive audience to convey what you've learned from your research is the academic equivalent of "preaching to the choir" with none of the implied criticism that this phrase carries. Rather, they are a ready audience with opportunities to translate from the classroom to practice.

Finally, think about professions. We have already noted that general management is not currently, and may never, be recognised as a profession. Nevertheless, a range of accrediting and professional bodies do circulate at both the level of general management and sub-disciplines such as project management, marketing, logistics, etc. Working in partnership with such intermediary bodies to conduct research and feed that research back into mandatory curricular expectations offers one of the most compelling routes to highly impactful research simply because you extend your reach beyond your own classroom and into the classrooms of all those students studying to become accredited or affiliated with the professional body concerned. Conceptualised narrowly as a logical, linear progression from theory to practice, current views of impact risk overlooking processes and actors who are central to the more diffuse, relational and temporally dispersed ways in which the four types of impact we set out here can, and does, occur. The differing opportunities for impact set out here, can be mapped (see Figure 2.1).

Having created the opportunity for impact to occur through people, places and professions, we will move on to consider performativity and the ways in which theory is enacted (in Chapter 3) and the ethical considerations of impactful research (in Chapter 5).

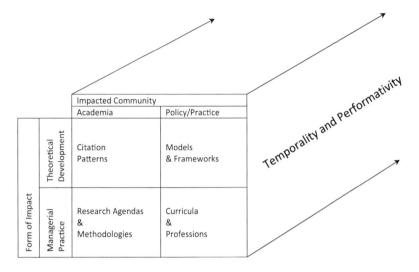

Figure 2.1 Impact map

Notes

1 The first Research Assessment Exercise (RAE) was conducted in 1992 and has been repeated in 1996, 2001, 2008, 2014 and 2021.
2 Private communication with senior business school figures in the US.

3 Conceptualising impact as theory in use

The impact agenda is an agenda driven by key sponsors of research – business, government and research agencies – that suggests the need for new ways of working and researching in business and management. This chapter conceptualises impact by considering broader understandings of what it means to use theory in practice. In so doing, we first explore the latest thinking on the *performativity* of theories. We discuss the implications of performativity theory for our unfolding understandings of *theory in use* and argue that a performative view reframes the relationship between theory and practice. This performative approach is found to be helpful in the development of new approaches for the production and consumption of theory and so our efforts to address the "impact agenda". In sum, we ask: *what are the implications of performativity theory for the way we approach the development of impactful research?*

Theories as performative artefacts with agency

Back in 2015, a Special Issue of the *Journal of Marketing Management* explored the performativity of marketing and market studies theories and reflected on the implications of performativity research for those seeking to develop their "impactful research" agendas (Mason et al., 2015). The introductory paper in the Special Issue explored the relevance of performativity theory for the field of marketing, tracing the term "performativity" to Austin's (1962) concept of "performative utterances"; speech acts that instead of simply describing an existing reality, through their utterance, perform that reality. A well-known example is the statement *I now pronounce you husband and wife*, which, if uttered in the right context, will produce "husband and wife". Austin called this an illocutionary effect. As the authors note, Austin did not only consider speech acts in isolation but also, critically, made much of the specific contexts or *situations* within which specific speech acts were performed. The combination of speaking and doing in context has been widely referred to as situated practice (Mason and Spring, 2011; Mason, 2012; Keating et al., 2014); an observation we return to in Chapter 4. An important implication for understanding *theory in use* is the notion of theory as a specific form of conceptual, abstract knowledge that takes on new and precise meaning when it becomes situated in specific practices (at a specific place and time, with specific actors and socio-materialities). Situated practice assumes that theories in use are affected by and bring about different types of effects, because of their setting, situation or context. Context then, as highlighted in Chapter 2, really matters for *theories in use*. Different theories are likely to be used differently, in different contexts.

First introduced as a route to impact in management and organisational studies by Chris Argyris in the 1970s (Argyris, 1996), *theories in use* in a specific context have been linked with the need to be pragmatic (cf. Mason and Araujo, 2020). Indeed, Austin's core argument made use of the work of a group of scholars known as the *American Pragmatists* and, particularly, the work of John Dewey (1933). Dewey was concerned with what it means to know something and the role of language, action, *inter*action and *trans*action in generating knowledge and knowing in real-world, practical contexts. He argued that the practices of knowing (speaking, acting, interacting) are what helps actors inquire into *perplexed and trying situations* and that such inquiries reveal *new productive possibilities* (Dewey, 1938) or theories for future action. Austin drew on these ideas to argue that performativity produced perlocutionary effects, which can only occur under the right, "felicitous conditions". Butler (2010) illustrates the power of perlocutionary effects:

> A politician may claim that 'a new day has arrived' but that new day only has a chance of arriving if people take up the utterance and endeavour to make that happen. The utterance alone does not bring about the day, and yet it can set into motion a set of actions that can, under certain felicitous circumstances, bring the day around.
>
> (pp.147–148)

Notably, the felicitous conditions here are generated by *inter*action, specifically the response from the audience. The success of a perlocutionary performative is thus dependent on external conditions "that [do] not immediately or necessarily yield to the efficacy of sovereign authority" (Butler, 2010: 151). This notion of a sovereign authority is particularly important for organisation and market studies. Many organisational and market phenomena (e.g. employment norms, pricing patterns) exercise performative agency but are not "uttered" by a single subject; there is no sovereign authority. Rather they rely on networks of social relations, institutionalised practices and technological instruments (Butler, 2010; Austin, 1962). In considering performativity in market, management and marketing settings, the idea of perlocutionary effects thus seems particularly pertinent. Such effects necessitate a sequence of events that first produce the felicitous conditions.

Recently, the notion of *translocution* has been introduced as a core component of performativity (Palo et al., 2020), to explain the work required to produce felicitous conditions. That is, actors manage to put key contextual elements in place, through deliberate, purposive and skilful work. It is this work that generates felicity. Translocution, quite literally means "talking across". Much of this managerial work is discursive, dialogic, and concerned with working out what needs to be done. This observation positions reflexivity (see Chapters 1 and 4) at the heart of theory in use. The claim here is that managerial work is performed through translocution – where managers talk across abstract concepts and theories, multiple forms of expertise and the socio-technical-economic materialities of their situation (Palo et al., 2020). In this way, abstract concepts and theories become anchored in specific socio-material realities; they become resituated from the pages of a book or journal article into the messy complex multidimensional socio-technical world of action. The world is changed and re-organised by the use of the theory in practice, to guide practice and to guide the organisation of new and felicitous socio-material arrangements. But importantly, as theories are put into practice, they are also *changed* by practice. Elements of the theory that are not practical, misfire, create overflows of new knowledge and understanding meaning compromises have to be reached, and work-arounds generated. From this messy reality, new theories of action are produced (see Figure 3.1). A key observation here might be that theories themselves are reflexive, reflecting and re-presenting the new meanings and understandings co-produced through these dialogues and interactions.

A central facet of performative approaches, then, is the attention paid to how activities, practices, doings and sayings are conceptualised and re-presented, and then in turn, how they are reflexively used to bring about change in a particular situation or sites of practice in an iterative and ongoing cycle of action, interaction and transaction. These theoretical developments in the organisation and market studies literature have been collectively referred to as the "performative turn" (Gond et al., 2016).

Since before the market and organisational studies "performative turn" (Gond et al., 2016), the notion of performativity has been used in different fields of study, in slightly different ways (Bateson, 1972; Bourdieu, 1982; Derrida, 1991; Goffman, 1974; Latour, 1986; Lyotard, 1979; Cochoy et al.,

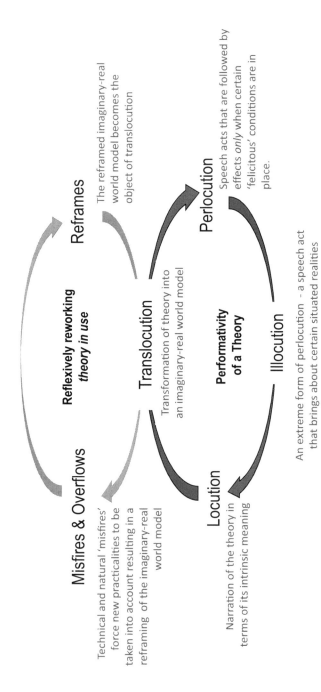

Figure 3.1 The iterative process of performativity

2010), but two contemporary research streams stand out as having particular relevance for how we understand *theories in use* and their impact.

The first stream derives from Butler's (1990) conceptualisation of gender, not as a fixed category (i.e. male/female) but as *performance* (i.e. how actors *do* or *perform* gender in practice). This approach, widely adopted in critical management studies (Maclaran et al., 2009; Spicer et al., 2009; Tadajewski, 2010), is particularly important for understanding the performativity of organisational, market and management theories because of its recognition of the variation in "performative intent" between different knowledge production and dissemination efforts (Fournier and Grey, 2000, also see, Law, 2004). Organisational, market and management theories and models often intend to have (positive) consequences for some actors; they are not simply describing an external reality, but they are presented with transformation in mind. This is important because the intent an actor has when picking up a theory or model is likely to affect *how* that model is used in practice and consequently the effects and outcomes it brings about. This can present challenging situations and even ethical dilemmas for academics; as foregrounded in Chapter 5, academics do not have control over where and how their theories are picked up and used or for what purpose.

The second research stream has developed in economic sociology, where Callon (1998) popularised the concept of performativity, claiming that "economics, in the broad sense of the term, performs, shapes and formats the economy, rather than observing how it functions" (p. 2). Callon takes economics to include theories, ideas, people, skills and techniques but the same claims can be held across organisational, market and management studies (see e.g. Palo et al., 2020; Aspers, 2007; Cochoy et al., 2010; Cochoy, 1998; Kjellberg and Helgesson, 2006). Although the notion of performativity is not new, few empirical studies have so far addressed how organisational, management or market theories are used and "performed" in practice (but see Part II of the edited volume by Zwick and Cayla (2011) for some notable exceptions).

The need for a deeper understanding of the practical use of organisational, market and management theories takes their cue from a long-standing, yet relatively under-researched critique of the mainstream literature. This includes concerns with what is often referred to as the gap between theory and practice (Hunt, 2002; Jaworski, 2011; Cornuel et al., 2009) that we raised in Chapter 1 and discussed in Chapter 2. The critique holds that theories are developed in ivory towers for academic journals and are irrelevant to and not useful for practitioners. In contrast, from a *theory in use* and *performativity* perspective, the theory – whether it be organisational, market or management – is seen an epistemological tool that is: (1) part of practice (i.e. in use), (2) representing a particular form of abstract knowledge and (3) open to change and adaptation through its use. A theory is, therefore, a performative artefact with agency and its agency (and so performative effects) depends on the skills, networks, materialities and expertise of those that use it in their situated practice. This means that when we do collaborative research *with* practitioners, policymakers and public groups, we both begin to understand the theory a new as it becomes resituated in its new setting, through the interaction and dialogue – the translocation – that talks across the different expertise and experiences that are brought to bear on its resituating. We return to the role of translocation and dialogue in Chapter 4, but we now turn to explore the implications of performativity theory for the study of the world and for further developing impactful theories for use in practice.

Implication of performativity theory for the impactful researcher

The conceptualisation of *theory in use* as performative, produced with intent and with transformation in mind (Callon, 2009), has significant implications for the way we think about impactful research. Because performativity theory makes no separation between theory and practice, theory is produced through understandings of practice and changed by new and resituated understandings of practice. From this purview, *there is no theory-practice gap to study*. Rather, there is a need to study *theories in use*; what are engaged-researchers, managers, organisations, key stakeholder groups doing *with* theories through their practice, why and with what outcomes? We argue that if our research is to be impactful, at the very least, we have to study, through our own and through practitioners' own reflexive practice, *theories in use*. Further, this study must consider theory and knowledge production *and* consumption and the relationship between the two: a point raised in Chapters 2 and 5 of this book. This duality of this perspective has four important implications for how we consider impactful research practice:

1 it requires management researchers to adopt a position of equality in value of theoretical and practical knowledge.
2 it suggests the need for researchers to theorise *with* multiple theory users.
3 it frames the way we approach learning and teaching *theory in use* in different settings.
4 it influences the way management researchers approach their development of research proposals for funding which has impactful research and impact designed-in to its conception.

It is valuable to explore each of these implications in turn.

Equality in value of theoretical and practical knowledge

First, performativity theory and its grounding in a practical rationality suggests that theory in use has a flat ontology. That is, it assumes that there is no hierarchy between different forms of knowledge and expertise. This means providing a parity between not just actors, knowledge and socio-material and technical things that produce knowledge but also, additionally, the types of knowledge produced and consumed by different knowledgeable actors (experts) and their normalised practices of knowledge production and consumption.

Because practical rationality regards knowledge as a set of sociocultural practices situated in, and inextricably linked to, the socio-material conditions in which it is produced and used (Hassard and Kelemen, 2002; Knorr Cetina, 2010), the impactful researcher needs to recognise the multiple forms of knowledge and expertise within their sites of inquiry – the researcher and the manager; the lit-re-view and inter-view. Each expert acts as a knowledge producer *and* user, in the collaborative, engaged or action research context. The theorising practices of these different experts are, however, different. Researchers, for example, focus on producing theoretical knowledge by combining literature with empirical observations of practice in the pursuit of new theories or the refinement of existing ones and consume knowledge through work on research panels, journal boards, peer reviewers and readers of published and unpublished literature that develops and grows through time (Hassard and Kelemen, 2002). In contrast, practitioners tend to produce practical knowledge grounded in their managerial experience across multiple but specific organisational sites of practice and make use of information that decays through its use (stock market prices, e.g., are relevant at a specific point in time). While practitioner's knowledge has been called many different things – practical (Gherardi, 2006), practical judgement (Dunne, 2005), informal theory (Usher et al., 1997) and phronesis (Chia and Holt, 2008) – the consensus is that it constitutes knowledge that is specific to and embedded in practice. Thus, a practical knowledge is both representational and emergent, a condition and consequence of immersion in practice (Wagenaar, 2004).

It follows then that *theory in use* has multiple meanings (Abend, 2008), combines different forms of knowledge, and gives each form a parity and voice both in the field and on paper. What happens with the resituating of a theory from paper into practice (or from one setting to another) is impacted by the particularity of the socio-material-political arrangements already in place. Thus, by giving equality to these different forms of knowledge and knowing, the impactful researcher is much better positioned to be open to critique (Argyris, 1996), theoretical misfires in practice and to alternative theoretical possibilities, as well as to critique research practice, enabling findings to be much more open to scrutiny and debate (Weick, 1989) in real-time. This suggests that the impactful researcher is more likely to inhabit the world of abductive reasoning, *in vivo* experimentation (cf. Muniesa and Callon, 2007) and theoretical iteration rather than the positivistic world of theorise and test.

Theorising with multiple theory users

Second, performativity theory suggests the need for the impactful researcher to theorise *with* (not just from) practitioners and other interested stakeholders. This suggests a specific type of case research with deep immersion in complex real-world problems (Argyris, 1996; MacLean et al., 2002). From this purview, a specific kind of researcher and practitioner theorising follows. The challenge in theorising with practitioners is the very different needs for different forms of outcome: for researchers, there is the need to generalise; for practitioners, there is a need to be specific and concrete *in situ*. Tsoukas's (2019: 1) foregrounds the researcher's "craving for generality" from what he calls "small-N studies" – in-depth, rich, ethnographic descriptions of particular sites of action. Drawing on Wittgenstein, Tsoukas (2019: 386) argues that this is a process of analytical and conceptual refinement:

> the distinctive theoretical contribution of small-N studies stems from seeing particular cases as opportunities for further refining our hitherto conceptualization of general processes. Specifically, particular cases share family resemblances rather than an overarching feature. Concepts are empirically under-determined. Theorizing is an analogical process (Vaughan, 2014): small-N studies researchers notice analogies with processes described in other studies and, in an effort to account for the specificity of the particular case under study, they draw new distinctions and, thus, further refine what is currently known. Without the specificity of the particular case, new distinctions will not be possible.

The "particular" thus grounds observations and produces practical knowledge of a practice setting. Tsoukas makes a further observation about what it means to theorise using practical knowledge. By invoking the notions of concepts and conceptualisation work (also see, Mason et al., 2017), Tsoukas draws out the critical role of theoretical knowledge and a practically situated conceptualisation of the theory itself:

> without the aid of hitherto available conceptualizations, conceptual refinement will be limited .... the craving for generality is not the craving for subsuming particular instances under general laws or mechanisms,

but the craving for a clearer view – higher elucidation (Schaffer, 2016). The analytical refinement achieved does provide general concepts, which, however, are inherently open-ended – generalizations are heuristic. They aid generic understanding without annihilating the epistemic significance of the particular.

(Tsoukas, 2019: 386)

Our aim then is through an abductive reasoning process performed *with* practitioners, the *researching-practitioner* and the *practicing-research* (Cunliffe, 2002, 2003, 2004) can together produce multiple views of a problem and open up opportunities to find multiple ways of declaring a set of descriptive observations as cases of something through multiple iterations between concepts and empirical observations (Ragin and Becker, 1992). Concepts here are not drawn from theory as fully formed entities; instead, they are "open-ended constructions that are not fully defined a priori, nor are they connected to the empirical world in a definite manner (Weick, 1989: 519), but are partly determined through the particular practices in which they are enacted" (Shotter and Tsoukas, 2011: 336). By stressing that concepts are open to situational uniqueness and refinement, theorising *with* practitioners creates opportunities for practitioners and theorists. For practitioners, theoretical concepts can be used "as a telescope or microscope to look through to see new 'openings' in their practices for their further development, refinement and (perhaps) correction" (Shotter and Tsoukas, 2011: 337). For theorists, casing provides an opportunity to learn from practitioners on the specificities of empirical settings as well as help them situate observations in a broader class of phenomena through the use and refinement of theoretical concepts (Wieviorka, 1992). When this happens, a new language of knowledge exchange and translocution can occur, thus avoiding some of the traps and challenges of knowledge and translation so vividly described by Bartunek (2020).

Learning and teaching theory-in-use in different settings

Third, performativity theory suggests the need for academics and practitioners to learn how to use and work with theories (and thus, theorise) *in situ* and in multiple and different settings. In Chapters 1, 2, 4 and 5, we foreground the responsibilities of academics to support management learning in the classroom as a prime site of research impact. With both responsible research and impact in mind, the need to expand understandings of what it means to use theory seems pertinent. The careful use and potential abuse of theories, as well as the responsible selection of the right theories to teach (Ghoshal, 2005) must all be part of the cannon of the impactful researcher.

Indeed, the original idea behind the Harvard Case Method (HCM) was to treat the classroom and the case study as a safe experimental space where management and organisational students could try out their theories and see what different theoretical lenses enabled them to see and the judgements they enabled them to make, with all their limitations (cf. Bridgman et al., 2016). Recent critiques of the HCM suggest that this learning method has moved away from its origins but efforts to provide places and spaces for those studying management to experiment with theories in use seems critical and only likely to expand the understanding of both teaching-researchers and learners. As the combination of theoretical and practical knowledge and judgement involves an ability to classify situations in ways that go beyond the habitual, it broadens what counts as experience (Usher et al., 1997; Dunne, 2005) and is expansive. But, as practical knowledge is not confined to cognition, it also affords opportunities for researchers to observe what managers (and managers in the making) actually do as they make use of our theories in their practice and in their practicing. Because practical knowledge is embodied and enacted knowledge and is never fully or even never likely to become codified (Wagenaar, 2004), we will, as researchers, always be in pursuit of opportunities to observe. This understanding of knowledge and knowing has essential implications for understanding how managers can learn to reflect and theorise through the performance and adaptation of theory in use.

The bidirectionality of learning (between practitioner and researcher; between researcher and policymaker) is worthy of further reflection. Outside of the classroom, in the research field, the same observations hold. Each and every time, we have engaged with a new site of inquiry, even when equipped with well-used theoretical toolkits, we have always learned something new. This phenomenon is widely reported by those discussing collaborative, action and engaged research approaches (MacLean et al., 2002). The bidirectional nature of continuous learning through the treatment of theories as always and necessarily in the making because they encounter new settings is an observation similarly made in Chapters 2, 4 and 5 in this book.

Funding impactful research

Making social science research valuable by attaching it to STEM (Science, Technology, Engineering and Mathematics) research and to technical and social innovation through the framing of *grand challenges* is likely to be central to securing the resources needed to achieve impact at scale. As we have seen in Chapters 1 and 2, theories do not perform in isolation. They need to be attached to greater political movements and the desire for change.

As others have shown, they require significant resources. Bartunek (2020: 20) describes three cases of impact achieved through research, for example:

> CFPB was based on Warren's theorizing that regulatory bodies were necessary to keep many large financial institutions from carrying out unethical processes that harmed consumers. Its primary actor was Elizabeth Warren, but the many other actors included the U.S. Congress, U.S. Presidents and their appointees, employees of the CFPB, and financial institutions whose profitability would depend at least in part on the regulations being enacted. The primary activities involved getting the CFPB signed into legislation and developing its components and the CFPB itself. The materials the CFPB made available to American citizens and the positive assessment by Peterson (2016) were among its material artifacts. However, there was and is not unanimous agreement with Warren's theory, especially on the part of financial institutions and the current presidential administration.

In each case, the theoriser/researcher has turned activists and done much more than represent research insights theoretically. They have intervened at great expense, often removing themselves from normal academic life. There are of course examples of significant management and organisational research impact where researchers have remained in academic life, but as the Research Excellence Framework's 2014 published impact cases show – those that tend to achieve impact tend to have the resources to do so. Significant research resources (typically £1m+) tend to achieve significantly more impact than unfunded projects. This is perhaps not surprising, especially as the sponsoring organisations only award funding to those research projects that have significant impact reach designed-in to their projects. But there is an important point here. The UK in particular (less so in Europe and in the USA) has suffered from a catastrophic lack of investment in business and management research investment in recent years – a point made in Chapter 1 and reported by the Chartered Association of Business Schools Report (2020). This means that researchers can only achieve impact on a limited scale through those they directly engage. This is requiring a fundamental shift in the way we think about research, research teams and the interdisciplinary nature of research in action.

The research funding landscape has other implications for impactful researchers. Much of the business management research that does get funded is funded as part of STEM-driven bids, where business and management research is treated as an "implementation science". This can create huge pressures on those business and management researchers learning to engage with the STEM disciplines, and those the partnering business and policymakers within the research setting, to create enough common ground to make the project a genuinely interdisciplinary and productive space. For many business and management scholars, this means significant investments of time and energy to learn the language of new disciplines and research settings and contexts. Additionally, such interdisciplinary, grand challenge projects can compromise what theories can be performed and put to use, and how insight on their development and transformation can be captured and recorded for a broader audience. Such programmes, especially those involving many research partners (SMEs, practitioners and policymakers), are often fast-paced and do not sit easily with the routines of academic life and the teaching calendar. Yet, when this type of grand challenge projects can be made to work, the outcomes can be impressive. In Chapter 6, we describe Lancaster University's RECIRCULATE project that has worked with African researchers and villagers to create clean water systems, maintained by entrepreneurs that now earn a living from the socio-economic benefits created by them, within their communities. All this suggests that funding and time to do impactful research is critical, if we are to achieve impact at scale.

Conclusion

In sum, using performativity theory to open up how we understand what impactful research practices look like, and how we perform them through *theory in use* (whether we begin by using our own theories or the theories of others), offers us valuable insights into what to expect as researchers. It suggests that engaged research and the purpose of intervention require close and often continued collaboration, theorising with others who have very different but complementary practices of knowledge production and consumption and often, significant resources including researcher time and income. Working as impactful researchers we expect to theorise *with* practitioners, policymakers and those from other often unrelated disciplines and to develop at least, in part, some new and shared practices and language of knowledge exchange and production/consumption. These new performative researching–theorising practices will smooth the way for making both abstract and concrete change.

4 A model of dialogue for co-production of practice-oriented learning and impact

In this chapter, we will argue that dialogue is an essential process in constructing impact. An exchange-based view of dialogue holds that thoughts and practices can be explained and exchanged between people, and while this can be an important first step, our contention is that this is not sufficient to enable deep and lasting change in practice. Lasting change in practice requires learning: sometimes for a step in improvement, sometimes for a transformational shift and sometimes for reflecting on the learning process and one's role within it (Brockbank et al., 2002). Brockbank et al. argue that dialogue is fundamental in practice-oriented learning of incremental, transformational and processual types because little or no learning can truly be achieved in complete monologic isolation. Learning requires a context and the input of stimuli, inspirations, problems and counter-views and these sources of input for the learner often exist in interaction with others. The others can interact directly in person or indirectly through reading, observing or listening.

The process of practice-oriented learning means that the learner has to be able to understand the external input and work with it to produce their own outcome. The learning activities of discovering, internalising, adapting, rejecting and refining all entail some connection between the self and the other. This perspective implies, therefore, that learning to improve or change practices incorporates a process in which there is an encounter between people, ideas and practices such that knowledge and skill are changed (Beech, 2017), and impact-oriented dialogue is an enabling process within such learning. In order to be successful, this also implies an attitude of openness to learning: less a hope that, through conversing, my ideas will change those of others and more an willingness to being changed oneself through reflexivity (Beech, 2008). The levels of learning discussed here relate to the levels of impact discussed in Chapter 1, with changes in the immediate context relating to the application of new skills or knowledge and meta-level impact relating to broader social learning, for example, as a person takes their new skills into another new environment or as researchers develop new methodological insights that they can apply in future projects, or which other researchers can apply.

In Chapter 1, we defined impact as "evidenced change occurring as a result of the purposeful application of co-developed knowledge". This definition makes explicit a focus on knowledge that is practical – that is, which regards theory as a way of picking up learning from one context and using it as either inspiration or broad prescription for action in another setting and which seeks to build knowledge inductively from experience. Therefore, the approach is explicitly both theoretical and practical, and dialogue is not only between individuals but also between ways of generalising practice into the future – either through theories, "best practice" examples, protocols, frameworks or through the skills that practitioners develop and apply in new situations.

One of the interesting debates in practice theory (e.g. Nicolini, 2012) is the question of how practices move – over time within a context or between contexts (e.g. ideas which improved manufacturing being used to improve services and "Lean processes" or global companies which seek to transfer practices from one geographical (and cultural) setting to another, often with mixed results). These issues are discussed in more detail in Chapter 3. It is often the case the practices and ideas change and adapt as they "travel" between different organisational, professional, cultural and temporal contexts. As discussed in Chapter 1, there is a variety of platforms through which ideas and practices travel and all of them include an initiator – often an author or a practitioner – and an agent who picks up the inspiring idea. The agent may need to consciously adapt ideas to fit a new context or sometimes their inventiveness is not deliberate but comes from an inadvertent reinterpretation of a codification of practice as it is interpreted in a different (organisational) culture. For some, this "dilution" of "best practice" can be seen as a problem – particularly, where consistency (e.g. in the quality of a product) is highly valued. Alternatively, and particularly where practices relate to services and processes, this agential form of learning and adapting (treating the original as an inspiration for new or refined ideas rather than something that must be slavishly imitated) can be creative and productive. This aspect of dialogue relates to the concept of translocutions, discussed in Chapter 3.

Our understanding of practice is that it is not simply behaviour but is meaningful behaviour, which is imbued with the significance of the culture in which it occurs (Gherardi, 2000). Practice relates to memory, ideas, feelings, experience and cultural learning, and so, if it is to be effective, dialogue has to be a means of connecting at these deeper and more interwoven levels. Thus, dialogue is both deeply social and deeply personal (Beech, 2008).

> [O]ur thoughts and ways of living are often not only our own.
>
> (Isaacs, 1999: 302)

For Isaacs, part of an enabling dialogue is to understand our "inner ecology" of feelings and thoughts. He sees thoughts and feelings as distinguishable but interwoven. Feelings, such as feeling anxious or hopeful, occur in a context of meaning in which patterns of thought play a framing role. The feeling of anxiety is embodied as we have a physical reaction and relates to what we understand to be an anxiety-producing circumstance, for example, where our ability to influence events is outstripped by other factors (Boudens, 2005; Troth, 2018). This thinking pattern entails predictive thinking about the future, assessment of risk and conceiving consequences, and these thoughts reflect our cultures and how we have learned about risk, reward, determinacy and agency. For Isaacs, a distinguishing feature of the inner ecology is that thoughts and feelings are mediated by interpretation, and although interpretation is at one level essentially personal, it is also culturally influenced. If dialogue is to be effective, there needs to be a way of connecting the inner ecologies of the people involved. Given that one person cannot directly reach inside another's head, our model emphasises mutuality, self-change in response to others and a series of dialogic activities undertaken in a hybrid community.

Arresting moments, difference and affirmation

Greig et al. (2012a) argue that thinking about impact has often been dominated by a knowledge transfer model: one in which "best practice" is transferred from a knowledge-site to a practice-site through a process of translation. The key activity in the knowledge-site is abstraction while the key activity in the practice-site is implementation. Abstraction can occur either by there being a research phase which is remote from the arena of practice or by data gathering within the practice-site and then undertaking analysis separately. The outcome can be a commodification of knowledge in which a template or ideal type is produced to be reproduced in new settings. Greig et al. argue that even in tightly controlled circumstances, there is a process of interpretation, adaptation and improvisation when putting knowledge into practice. That is, it is an active process that is not merely translating but also creating a new version of the practice. Their research indicates that even where the same terminology is used, for example, in a national organisation operating in multiple sites, significant differences emerged in "implementation". Further, they show that this active knowledge/ practice construction is fundamental to improving performance and in complex settings is preferable to merely imitative learning. Greig et al. show, for example, how "best" practices in healthcare were encapsulated in policy – a process of abstraction and reduction and then "rolled out" across three sites: a large city, a region including a city and surrounding districts and a rural area. In each case, the policy was implemented and was evaluated as having several notable successes. However, in their analysis, it was clear that the same practices were not being enacted. The way that multi-disciplinary health teams interacted varied considerably as some were in purpose-designed health buildings with extensive facilities, administration and professional staff who operated within specialties, whereas others in a rural area mainly operated alone, in the homes of patients or in small cottage hospitals and covered a range of health and social care activities when visiting patients and their families.

Similarly, Aston et al. (2019) found that best practices in policing management, whilst apparently adhering to the same policies (such as "stop and search") actually varied significantly between urban and rural settings. They argue that such variation is a strength and that to have simply demanded conformity (or the appearance of conformity) would have been ineffective and damaging to community relations in the rural areas. The nature of policing in urban areas is significantly different in that adopting practiced protocols was usually more effective, whilst in rural settings where police officers and the young people being stopped often knew each other, a more relationship-based approach was appropriate. However, given the nature of evaluation and measures of practices against numerical targets, there was also a macro-practice of reporting that gave the appearance of implementation being the same in different areas. In the discursive construction, this enabled "evidence-based" decision making and "comparative analysis" of performance while underlying this appearance were actually significant differences in the nature of the practices. The need to provide an appearance of a practice and its implementation relates to the concept of performativity which was discussed in greater depth in Chapter 3. Conversely, explorations of leadership and management in the police service have found that where authoritarian and controlling styles of leadership are applied problems arise in commitment, organisational learning and opacity of communications – as would be expected from the research on leadership practice in other industries (Beech et al., 2015).

It has long been recognised that involvement and participation are influential on the outcomes of efforts to bring about change. In Coch and French's (1948) classic study of change in a clothing factory, one group or workers were informed of changes to their job, while a second group were involved in discussions about how the working methods could be improved and unnecessary activities reduced. The first group immediately exhibited lower productivity, lower moral and increased grievances. In contrast, the second group adapted with the changes. This process may not have quite lived up to Isaacs' definition of dialogue as "a collective inquiry into the processes, assumptions and certainties that compose everyday life" (1993: 25), but it is likely that the level of engagement and potential for workers to influence the change is at least part of the explanation of the difference between the two groups.

This chimes with a relational perspective on organisations and impactful business and management research. Gergen (2009) has argued for a reversal of the traditional hierarchy between research and practice. He is critical of a view of research as being composed of a primary act of private writing and a secondary act of reporting findings:

> [the traditional approach is] First it is important that 'I know', and then it might also be helpful if 'I would tell others.' From the standpoint of relational being, we may properly reverse the hierarchy. That is, knowing comes into existence only through social participation. Acts of research only become intelligible . . . . through a relationship that precedes the acts themselves. . . . 'I speak with others, and therefore I can know'.
>
> (2009: 229)

Gergen et al. (2004) have argued that organisations are essentially relational. Impactful change in practice is not simply an exchange between but a function of relationships. It relates to how groups make sense of a situation with each other, how they make sense of the others and consequently how they act. For Gergen et al., this entails a process of relational coordination and they develop a perspective on generative dialogue which underpins this process.

A starting point to this process is to establish the dialogue between participants as "respectful equals" (Cunliffe, 2002). This entails recognising and valuing difference and seeing the practice/knowledge construction as a crafting process during which different types of skill are brought to bear (Greig et al., 2012b). Working out what to pay attention to in the dialogue is crucial in how this mutual respect is enacted. Greig et al. (2012b) argue that this entails noticing and holding onto "arresting moments". Arresting moments are usually disruptive: they are the times when things that were previously taken for granted now stop making sense or appear in a new light. When members of a community of practice are in dialogue with each other, they are discussing practices *in situ* or from the "inside" and thus there can be a tendency to produce and reproduce embodied practices (Gherardi, 2009). However, where there is a relationship of difference, for example, when a research community and a practice community interact, articulating "insider" accounts to the other can reveal (both to the self and the other) unrecognised assumptions, gaps and surprises. There can be a temptation to gloss over such things as they can feel like an inadequacy in the account, a gap in one's professional knowledge, but these are the very "imperfections" that allow for generative learning. It is crucial to have an emotionally supportive context as it can be disconcerting and uncomfortable, but it is only by persisting in not resolving or glossing the matter that real creativity can occur. Greig et al. consider an example of musicians interacting with a producer. There is a difference over the inclusion and lyrics of a particular song on an album because of the lyrics being interpreted either as offensive (producer's perspective) or ironically critical of what they appear to be saying (musician's perspective). The situation ended up in a stand-off, but eventually the senior person became very emotional about the issue. While this was upsetting, it shocked people out of their established stances and out of their normal ways of being as a musician or a producer. The human connection of the emotion arrested the moment and made people stop and reconsider. This was the first step in them starting a dialogue in which they didn't just assume that they were right and the others were wrong (as usual). This example, if perhaps an extreme one, illustrates how an interruption to the normal flow of discussion can open up the possibility of self-change and greater reflexivity (a concept introduced in Chapter 1). Therefore, for Greig et al. (2012b), it is not only cognitive respect that the participants need for each other but also a "whole person" approach to supporting emotionally through the breaking down of past certainties and being resilient in concentrating on the unknown and the uncomfortable.

The element of difference between people, ideas and approaches is, for Gergen (2004), fundamental in productive dialogue. The meanings of single words depend on difference to other words for their meaning, for example, the word "bit" largely resembles the word "bat", but they mean quite different things. In dialogue, there is a shared process of constructing meaning and this too requires difference. Mere acceptance of the terms of the other, like mere rejection (e.g. condemning the other's utterance as unintelligible or simply wrong), brings the dialogue to a halt. Productive difference, the introducing of a new voice or perspective, or enquiring into the meaning of the other from a different standpoint enable the idea being discussed to be changed and enriched. This enriching occurs when sufficient bonds are created between the participants such that they move towards sufficient coherence which includes a combination of difference and affirmation.

Mason (2012) explores the development of a strategy and a new business approach to markets as a dialogical process and the practices she identifies of sensing and sense-making relate to difference and affirmation. She traces arresting moments of emotion in the dialogue when making a pitch for business the participants connect at an emotional level:

A1: so we pitch up to the company headquarters it's .... aaaaa-m-a-zzz-ing!....
K: wow

A1: .... And it's a lady that's running it. Wow. WOW! Just amazing in that culture. ...

K: she's good then

A1: Ah yes . . . . . so sharp, she's on the big issues straight away, she's terrific.

This arresting moment is noticeable, according to Mason, because it stands out from the expected culture and historical setting of the industry and so sensing is crucial, but this is clearly social rather than individual meaning making. A1 and K interact in a way which is not based on them having the same opinion but in sharing an interest in the dialogue such that overlaps between them become emphasised and later in the dialogue (not quoted here) new insights emerge. This occurs during sense-making practices in which interpretations of why a pitch had worked and how the nuances of interacting with customers in different cultures were handled.

Encountering the other and the self in scholarly dialogue

Anderson et al. (2017) raise a series of questions about our identities and how they relate to activities involved in impactful engagement. They argue that it can often be assumed that to have impact, the practitioners involved have to be senior (King and Learmonth, 2015), for example, senior executives who can change the strategy of a company or senior civil servants who can influence policymaking. However, "practitioner" is a broad identity category that may well include as much difference as it excludes. People who practice include, for example, part-time students as they are carrying out the activities of both studying and their employment. It is recognised that, although we might like to think that the employees of a company are strongly influenced by its strategy and leadership, in fact, there is a propensity for people to focus on their line managers and peers and their performance and experience of work related to these dyads and close work relationships (Clarke and Mahadi, 2017). So it could be argued that part-time student-practitioners who pick up ideas based on research and evidence and who seek to put those ideas into practice may have significant impact, albeit in a less headline-grabbing way than the introduction of a new policy or strategy might have. We might extend this argument to full-time students who may pick up ideas and activities in their study mode which impacts on their practice mode. For example, in entrepreneurial start-ups by graduates, there can often be a foundational idea, product or practice which has originated in study or in co-curricular activities (Astebro, 2012).

Anderson et al. (2017) also challenge us to rethink our academic identities when considering impact. Similarly, Knights and Clarke (2014) explore the tensions and challenges of a multifaceted academic profile. First, the discourse often relates to research impact, and while it is certainly true that the development of new knowledge in social sciences such as business and management can and does translate into practice, Anderson et al. argue that focusing only on the researcher aspect of our identities may inadvertently exclude a range of potential for impactful work. They refer to the "teaching-research nexus" as a site in which academics undertake activities that blur boundaries of what has been seen as distinct realms of knowledge-production and knowledge-dispersal. This can include "research-led teaching . . . research-informed teaching (teaching which is based on research) . . . and research-oriented (inquiry-based) teaching" (2017: 19). Their proposition is that an inclusive identity as a scholarly academic can include and blend a range of activities. Their thinking is based on Boyer's (1990) conception of a scholarship of integration. Boyer argues that there are four interrelated aspects of scholarship. These include: the scholarship of discovery which includes traditional research; the scholarship of integration which makes connections between concepts and disciplines; the scholarship of application which focuses on synthesis and the movement of ideas and practices into different knowledge-practice sites; and the scholarship of teaching which engages a broader group as students and scholars and hence expands the knowledgeable community.

If we consider the breadth of what academics actually do, particularly in business and management where it is common for there to be a blend of activities across the spectrum that Boyer identifies, it is clear that there are multiple opportunities to influence and to be influenced. Preparing for teaching commonly involves engaging with and understanding an area of literature and examples of practice, and it also involves understanding the process from the learner's perspective, that is, applying the activities of professional academic practice. Similarly, discovering new knowledge typically involves understanding a field and gaining data and/or insight which adds to that field, that is, applying the activities of professional academic practice. But these practices are not solo activities. Although there are solo elements to them such as reading and analysing, in fact, they are essentially relational in at least two facets. Firstly, they are relationally oriented. When an academic is undertaking solitary reading and thinking, they are actually engaging with the work of others and they are working with this input to produce something (a literature review, a lecture) which has the purpose of engaging others. So others are written into even the apparently solo activities of scholarship. Secondly, others are present and influential in many of the activities, from gathering data to conducting seminars and conducting case studies. The dynamic of thinking and inspiration is not mono-directional but flows between academics and practitioners/student-practitioners. Surprising questions and alternative perspectives can provide arresting moments in which we come to question a taken-for-granted assumption or throw light onto a new possibility.

For Bartunek (2007), this occurs in a form of relational scholarship in which it is possible to, "imagine a future in which academic-practitioner conversations and mutual relationships happen as a matter of course" (2007: 1330). Bartunek's concept of mutual relationships is of particular significance. In some forms of thinking about "knowledge transfer", the focus is on expertise and what thus constitutes a separation or difference between academics and practitioners. A danger with such identities of separation is that they can produce a hierarchical form of discourse in which "those who know" have the role of transmitting information and "those who practice" have the role of receiving and then trying to implement (MacIntosh et al., 2017). This social arrangement can militate against generative dialogue (Beech et al., 2010) and against mutuality in the relationship (Bartunek, 2007).

Mutually based dialogue is fostered more effectively where the identity roles of the participants are purposefully blurred. The purpose is reconstituted as co-production of knowledge/practice rather than transfer and a separation of roles into either a knowledge-focus or a practice-focus. One way of thinking about this is to see all participants as practitioners in a hybrid micro-community of inquirers. The shared hybrid practice is co-producing new insights which inform developments or changes in how work is carried out, and this hybrid practice is constituted by a set of activities. These activities can be thought of in five groups:

1   Empirical activities: carrying out the work, reporting and observing existing ways of working.
2   Analytical activities: analysing, reviewing, gathering data and examples and making comparisons.
3   Design activities: designing, improvising and constructing experimental and developmental ways of working.
4   Reviewing activities: reviewing developments and refining.
5   Reflecting activities: reflecting and considering insights and learning for work, relationships and processes.

The crucial thing from a mutuality perspective is that the roles taken are fundamentally about fostering learning for the group as a whole. As discussed in Chapter 2, this would be closer to Shotter's (2006) approach to thinking from within – "withness thinking" – than to thinking from the outside – "aboutness thinking". This means that where there is expertise, it is offered as a resource to the group and as are experience and skills in analysis, design and learning facilitation. For there to be effective mutuality "the stripes need to be left at the door", that is, our badges of authority are not particularly relevant or helpful to effective dialogue, but our skills and willingness to empathise with others, to listen and to contribute what is most helpful to the overall outcome are. Hence, the metaphor of "transfer" may be unhelpful in the way that it has sometimes been characterised as being based on the dependency of one party on another. Generative dialogue is about a shared process that leads to shared outcomes rather than "ownership" of commodified ideas which can be exchanged.

It is important for us to understand this in the social context of power which relates to impact (MacIntosh et al., 2012). Increasingly, there are pressures for academics who want to be promoted and score well in university and national assessments of research impact to show their own leadership of research which has influenced the practice of others. This may be appropriate in some disciplines, but in business and management, there is a different kind of complexity in which problems are normally "wicked" and entwined, alternative perspectives are viable and "best practice" has a habit of working in one context and failing in another. Therefore, there is a need for a fuller understanding of co-production of entwined knowledge/practice in which the role of the academic is in the process over time, includes ignorance and curiosity as well as knowledge, but is fundamentally about a scholarly approach that enables learning and change. This means that it is important to establish the internal context for dialogue and the external context in which it takes place. We will now explore the five dialogic activities identified earlier and implications for contexts.

Dialogic activities of co-production of knowing/practicing

The actors in effect form a micro-community with the purpose of developing knowledge/practice. The purpose can be quite specific, for example, in helping with a particular problem or exploiting an opportunity. It can be more diffuse, for example, in developing a leadership approach to develop an organisational culture. It is important for the actors to have an agreed purpose at the outset so that they can be explicit in their choices of action and be conscious of any changes or additions to the purpose over time. Such changes may not be problematic in the way that "mission creep" is thought of. Rather, they are often beneficial and relate to opportunities arising because of expanding knowledge and developing relationships in the micro-community. The activities are part of the overall practice of co-production and may occur in a sequence from empirical work to reflection but are more likely to iterate and move in multiple directions. For example, observing the empirical work entails some choices and in-the-moment analysis and new versions of carrying out the work will be likely to include elements of improvisational adjustments to design ideas. However, it is useful to pay attention to each activity during a dialogical process to ensure there is a sufficient balance between action, analysis, creativity and communication in the learning. The temporal aspects were discussed in detail in Chapter 2, and, in particular, the sometimes unpredictable and cyclical nature of sequencing in which, for example, publications can make a little impact initially but later have notable influence, or sequences in Action Research can vary between inductive and deductive. Figure 4.1 illustrates the relationship of the activities to the central practice of co-producing knowledge/practice or to phrase it in an active mode, knowing/practicing.

In a micro-community, the actors all participate in each activity, sometimes contributing a particular skill, contextual knowledge or experience and sometimes contributing support for the micro-community inquiry. Such

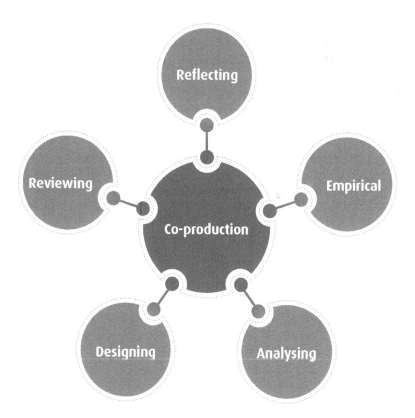

Figure 4.1 Dialogic activities of co-production of knowing/practicing

support can include facilitating questioning that draws out the expertise of others, making potential connections to analogous situations, and playing with ideas and experiments to open up creative possibilities. The mode in which these activities are undertaken has an ethical underpinning. For example, an academic can act in a consultancy mode (see Chapter 5) or in an Action Research mode (see Chapter 2) and ethical expectations can include competence, integrity and objectivity. These are discussed further in Chapter 5 and they raise questions for conduct. They also raise philosophical questions, for example, whether these interactive approaches are objective or subjective. Whilst much of the theory behind a dialogic orientation would be Interpretivist or Constructionist (Gergen, 2009), and hence question the idea of epistemological objectivity, the sense in which it is used ethically could be translated to mean that academics acting in a consultancy capacity should not act in a self-interested way to the detriment of others.

Empirical activities include carrying out the work in a learning mode. There are certain factors that can be helpful to pay attention to. These include the nature of the work, the tools and technologies used, how the work interacts with other processes or parts of a system, who undertakes the work and its adjoining activities (Blackler, 1993), and what helps and hinders. This can be the person who is doing the work paying particular attention to these observational points or other members of the micro-community can assist through observation and by questioning. It is typically difficult for a skilled worker to explicate details and connections that have become tacit knowledge for them, and it can be difficult for those embedded in the work practice to imagine alternatives because they are so used to the factors that hinder, form boundaries and which have become reified in a culture. Therefore, the role of others is particularly important in drawing out significance, tacit knowledge and assumptions that have become taken for granted.

Analytical activities are undertaken to deepen and broaden the thinking. The thinking can be deepened through focusing on the experiential data in analysis, questioning and highlighting connections and disconnections between the focal activities and other parts of a culture or system. The thinking can be broadened by looking outside the immediate environment and, for example, gathering examples from elsewhere, exploring industry trends and sometimes drawing inspiration from different settings or industries. This approach to analysis seeks to generate new possible insights, ideas and approaches which can feed into thinking about what might be changed.

Design activities are focused on developing changes to practice. These can be micro adjustments, complex macro projects or mezzo-level practices. In many cases, the micro, mezzo and macro are connected. For example, a macro change in leading a culture change towards greater agility and less formality could entail experimenting with how a particular meeting is run and the communications that go into, and come out of, the meeting. The design activities can discuss the specifics of behaviour, such as how the introduction should be phrased to encourage informality, and thinking about how such micro-actions can be experimental so that judgements can be made about how the action was received, what meanings were attributed to it and whether or not it helped move towards the macro aims. Design activities in co-production may not be deterministic but often leave some leeway for improvisation. Improvisation is a central skill in leadership and management as it is part of what makes leaders feel authentic to their colleagues and, given that leaders and managers are brought into play when there is no formulaic answer, there is often a creative element to leadership work. However, improvisation is not complete freedom. In fact, improvisation typically used well-rehearsed patterns and tropes which can be assembled in new ways at the moment (Kamoche and Cunha, 2001). Hence, design for improvisational and experimental practice can include accumulating resources, such as models, concepts, examples and methods, which can then be actively assembled and reassembled. This learning orientation including improvisation rarely implies mimetic behaviour in simply "adopting" best practice and more typically entails deconstruction and reconstruction of components.

Reviewing activities entail a checkpoint for action. They can be based on asking a series of "what if . . ." questions. For example, in thinking about running a meeting in a more informal manner to communicate an intention to work towards an agile culture, the actors may ask: "what if it is misinterpreted as weak leadership?" or "what if some people respond enthusiastically but others are clearly uncomfortable?" This kind of questioning helps the actor prepare for reentering the work situation, alert to key possibilities and with some preparation to engage with them. Sometimes "devil's advocate" questioning is adopted to test out design ideas critically. This can be helpful to identify reasons why the design idea might fail, unintentionally hinder progress or not achieve its purpose. It is important, however, that such questioning is seen as a group activity, not a role as if a person becomes identified as the devil's advocate in the group it is harder for them to play a natural role in generative and creative activities. It is also helpful for such questioning to be applied in a time-limited way as it inhibits creativity (Bilton and Cummings, 2010).

Reflecting activities before and after empirical activities are crucial for distilling learning and capturing it in a way that is memorable for the group and others who might benefit from the learning (Hibbert et al., 2010). Reflecting processes often include some individual work in advance of a meeting. The individual work includes considering insights on how the work or experiment went, how it connected to broader processes more or less effectively and how relationships (good or bad) were maintained or changed. Working as a group, the micro-community can then compare notes and insights, paying attention to both similarities and differences in interpretations. This activity also includes sufficient record keeping to make the learning explicit. In Chapter 5, we explore further Schön's (1983) exploration of reflective practice and his argument that the supposed opposition between rigour and relevance can be dissolved if we develop an epistemology of practice, and these reflective activities which can be undertaken alone but which can be enhanced in the right group context through the questioning and support of others. Such a setting can provide a good environment and stimulation for the kinds of arresting moments discussed earlier in this chapter.

In order for the micro-community to be able to learn and develop new ways of knowing/practicing a high level of trust is needed. If people are to display and explore uncertainties, failings and vulnerabilities as well as excitement, hopes and fears, they need to be in an environment where this is accepted and kept confidential. Being playful is part of creative thinking and, as this is often not part of organisational cultures, there needs to be a safe place for it to happen. When someone asks devil's advocate questions of an idea about which another person is passionate and excited, the conceptual difference can become personal. In addition, as such micro-communities bring together people with different skills, knowledge and ways of thinking, there needs to be an internal context that values difference and connectivity with "the other". Managing such an internal context takes some sophistication of leadership and interaction and it is a skill-set in itself (Beech, 2017). Doing this effectively can construct an environment similar to what Goffman (1958) imagines as the back-stage region where, away from the performance zone, actors can relate to each other with honesty and discuss the external environment in a way that they could not do in public. Time in the back-region can build up a reservoir of resilience that actors can draw upon when "on stage" or out in public.

While the micro-community can explicitly work on their internal context, they have to work within an external context, even if they are seeking to impact on it (Nguyen and Janssens, 2019). For example, in changing leadership style to influence a more agile culture, an actor is taking part in a popular discourse of leadership – what is seen as "strong", "ambitious" or "transformational" (Currie and Lockett, 2007; Lavine, 2014). Indeed, there is a broader context outside business and management which carries messages about what constitutes effective leadership, from sporting captains to political leaders and media representations of heroic leaders. Therefore, in making a change, careful consideration needs to be given to the pre-existing meanings and expectations that people will have. It may be helpful to make a contrast to a popular discourse explicit along with the reasons for making such a move. Such a debate on concepts would be welcomed in some organisational cultures. On the other hand, in some cultures, it works better to start by doing something differently and afterwards start to draw people's attention to it so that they are able to learn on the basis of their experience of the new approach rather than starting from a cognitive argument. Clearly, there are enormous complexities and connotations to understanding the impact of the external environment, but some understanding of how changes might be perceived and responded to is part of the co-production process.

Impact as collaborative practice: three approaches

Building on these dialogical activities of co-production, we can identify cycles of collaborative practice that combine some or all of the activities in alternative ways. Our view of collaborative practices is that they are a set of activities in which participants contribute to a collaborative venture to change something in the world for the better. It is a "team sport" in which different skills and know-how are brought to bear in crafting a process and outcomes, and this relies on relationships that are sufficiently trusting to enable learning, errors, changing minds and exciting discoveries. Over time, the roles and relationships of those in the collaboration can change and typically have an influence on each other. In part, this is because the boundaries of know-how become blurred as people learn skills from each other. Significantly, however, as a collaboration lasts over time, the participants become changed through their involvement – they begin to see the context and the practices from the perspective of the collaborative venture rather than their original starting point. We are not suggesting that all impact is like this, it remains the case that instrumental and contractual exchange can effectively bring about change in organisations, but in long-lasting impactful work, the relationships, processes and practices are all likely to be modified because of the engagement.

There can be a cyclical nature to such experiences. We are not suggesting that there are closed circles in which the participants arrive back at the same starting place but that a flow of practices moves in a cycle such that a new starting point is achieved for any second iteration. We are also not suggesting that the cycles are a one-way or absolute flow – there are many forwards and backwards movements, but the notion of a cycle of collaborative practices can help to display some of the imbricated processes such that participants can more overtly make choices about what they focus on and what skills they bring to the table. In the following examples, we provide generic descriptors of practices.

We describe three cycles of impactful work which represent different orientations and potentially different epistemologies. These are: designed-in impact, practice-based research and practice-as-research. These are abstract "ideal types" intended to help process (meta level) learning as academics and partners reflect on their own practice and make decisions about how to proceed in different settings.

Designed-in impact is an orientation with a rich tradition in social science. For example, variants of Action Research, Engaged Scholarship and Mode 2 work could operate in a cycle like this. The cycle starts with a dialogue about the inspiration for the work. This could be a problem or opportunity recognised in an organisation or, alternatively, be an experience or a reflection. The dialogue is between a participant from the organisational context and an external researcher whose expertise appears to be relevant. The dialogue can be a process of identifying, clarifying and defining the nature of the problem or opportunity to be addressed. The next step is the co-design of a research approach, experiment or intervention. The research skills are significant in the design and the know-how of the context is important in designing an approach that is implementable. The next step is to implement the design, to observe, experiment and adapt. This can involve both the researcher and the practitioner in collaborative action with each bringing complementary skills to bear. Next, there is a phase of review, evaluation and reflection in which a new cycle can be designed, for example, focusing on a refined version of the problem or in scaling up the approach developed. Throughout these stages, the identities remain distinct (researcher and practitioner) but there is an overt intention to work collaboratively (see figure 4.2).

In *practice-based research*, there is a focus on practices as meaningful events in which actors bring to bear their knowledge and skills, using their technology in a division of labour to produce an outcome that has particular meaning or significance in their culture. Hence, practices are not raw behaviour but are embedded in systems of meaning. Consequently, change is not only a technical matter, but it is also a socio-psychological matter, and impact needs to accommodate both if it is to be effective. The initial step of identifying a target practice to be changed entails an understanding of how it links to other practices and the social systems that support it. This is followed by a deeper analysis of the context, meaning (often multiple meanings for different stakeholders), technology and people factors involved in enabling and executing the practice. The dialogue and co-design are modifications to an aspect of the practice or potentially a new practice that either replaces the old one or enables systems to reform in a new way. The review step includes both the actions and meanings in their context, bearing in mind that both or either can change – for example, the action may

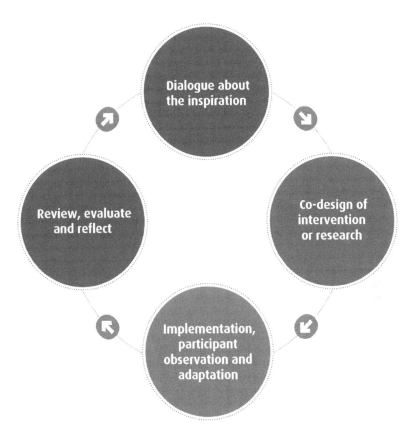

Figure 4.2 Designed-in impact

be changed in only a minimal way but the meanings associated with it can change considerably because of the process that has been experienced by the participants. The next step can be a new identification of the practice to be worked on or a different part of the practice network can be targeted. The roles in this approach start as distinct but often become blurred as researchers and practitioners become co-explorers of culturally embedded practices with some exploring more from the inside and others more from the outside, but over time, each can become affected by the interpretations of the other (see figure 4.3).

Our third ideal type is *practice-as-research*. Traditionally, this style of work has been more common in arts and creative practice but the orientation is increasingly being adopted through "in-residence" schemes where practitioners from one setting spend time in the setting of others, learning about it

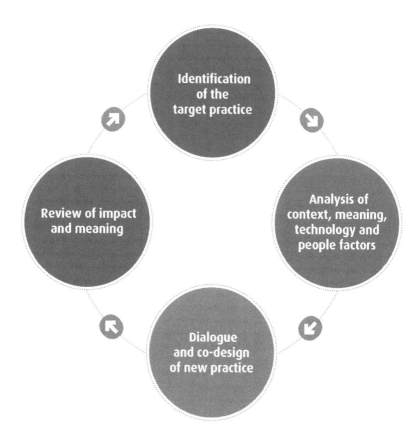

Figure 4.3 Practice-based research

initially with the perspective of an outsider, gradually becoming embedded and developing a hybridised insight of the insider–outsider. This cycle starts with a deliberate blurring of identities, for example, being a researcher-in-residence or a practitioner-researcher. As participants become embedded in the context, they learn about the culture and gain insight into what is normal for the members of the culture but which may be unusual or surprising to others. There can then follow an experimental approach to revealing their culture back to the organisation. This could be in the shape of exploring the consequences of particular practices or highlighting disjunctures between culturally accepted accounts of what works and observations of what actually occurs. If the researcher-in-residence or practitioner-researcher is sufficiently accepted in the culture, it is possible to raise and address challenging

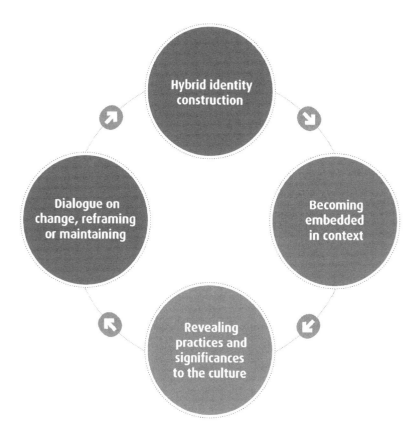

Figure 4.4 Practice-as-research

issues that members of the culture may or may not have been fully aware of. Equally, there can be a celebratory revealing of values or achievements that people can treasure. Hence, there is a dialogic step in which there are choices about changing a practice, reframing how it is understood or maintaining it with renewed value (see figure 4.4).

Conclusion

In order for impact to occur, change is necessary, and hence learning is necessary. Like Greig et al. (2012a), we acknowledge that sometimes this is managed by knowledge transfer and mimetic learning of "best practice", but for much of what concerns business and management greater creativity and agency are required. Where organisational issues are interconnected, dynamic and "wicked" they are less amenable to closed-system problem solving. In such situations, we have argued that dialogue is a core process for change. We have conceived dialogue as a way in which traditional identities, such as "academic", "researcher" and "practitioner" (Anderson et al., 2017), can be challenged in a productive way. Their very blurring can be productive in challenging unhelpful hierarchy (Beech et al., 2010) and separation of roles.

We have proposed a model in which micro-communities come together with a shared purpose at the same time as valuing their differences and what these differences enable them to contribute to the group effort – the sense of mutuality that Bartunek (2007) emphasises. Co-production lies at the heart of the model and its outputs (ranging from the specific to the pervasive) are new ways of knowing/practicing. We have outlined five activities that constitute the practice of co-production and have emphasised the need to manage the internal context of the micro-community to enable it to be productive. This is one way of connecting the inner ecologies of the people involved (Isaacs, 1999). This relies on an ethos of mutuality and a willingness to foster learning for the micro-community and the broader community as a whole. This holistic approach incorporates cognition, emotion and embodiment. It also incorporates values and ethics and it is to these matters we turn in the next chapter.

In summary, we have proposed that:

1   Given that impactful change is based on the application of co-developed knowledge, practice-oriented learning (to improve, transform or re-process) is a core constituent process in achieving impact.
2   Practice-oriented learning is dialogical in that it requires the learner to understand something about the context of the practice, alternative approaches and to be able to change one's knowledge skills and practice.
3   Practice-oriented learning can include memetic activity but more often entails adaptation and invention as practices translate between different organisational, professional, cultural and temporal contexts. Dialogue can enable this adaptation and creativity.
4   Dialogue can produce "arresting moments" in which there is a realisation of a different way of practicing. Such moments are often not only cognitive but also embodied in emotion and experience.
5   Dialogue underpins different types of scholarship which can produce new knowledge, new applications, new connections or expand the knowledgeable community through learning. Any of these types of scholarship (and any combination) can lead to impact.

6   Activities of co-production include work that is: empirical, analytical, designing, reviewing and reflecting. In a "flat hierarchy", each activity is valued and professionals and academics can act in micro-communities to contribute their skills to these activities.

7   Collaborative practices can be identified as virtuous cycles and these include: designed-in-impact, practice-based-research and practice-as-research.

5   Ethics of impact

As this book has shown by this point, impact is much more complex a term than is typically recognised. It incorporates multiple meanings, multiple relationships and multiple performances, typically over an extended period of time.

It is relatively rare, however, that impact is thought of in terms of its ethical dimensions. As previous chapters have shown, it is discussed much more frequently as something that is valuable for academics to do and for which they will be rewarded if they get it right, whatever that means in the context in which they are working. In the UK, this is likely to mean high ratings on the REF. In some universities in the US, it may mean expectations of posting regularly on social media, while also maintaining a stellar publication record in top-tier journals.

Yet, academic impact, like any persuasive activity, necessarily includes a number of ethical dimensions, many of which are intertwined. In this chapter, we will discuss several of them, including:

1   Ethical obligations of academics in relation to managers and other practitioners.
2   The characteristics of practitioners whom academics hope to be impacting and academics who may be better at connecting with them.
3   The means through which impact takes place, especially consulting and teaching.
4   The question of whether academic training is helpful or hurtful for practitioners.
5   The type of impact that is expected to occur.
6   Complications of translation of academic writing for practice.
7   The direction of impact.
8   On what topics should academics strive to have impact?
9   Some challenges of impact.

1. Ethical obligations of academics towards managers and other practitioners

Many academic associations include in their ethical codes that the obligations of academics towards the public. In the case of management-oriented organisations, this refers in particular to managers, policymakers and other practitioners.

For example, the British Academy of Management (BAM) statement of values[1] states that BAM: "Promote(s) the scholarly voice in policy and practice in order to influence national and local policy, educational provision, and the design and delivery of curricula (and) on the basis of high quality scholarship engage(s) with funders of research and other actors in the management field". It adds that "We aim to be inclusive, recognise and respect the diversity in our community, and promote high quality in all we do".

The code of ethical conduct of the Academy of Management (AOM)[2] spells out several ethical responsibilities that AOM members have towards managers and the practice of management and seems to assume that the standard ways that AOM academic members link with managers and other organisational members is through consulting. Consulting is typically not discussed in the impact literature (e.g. it hasn't been discussed to this point in our book), but it is an obvious means of impact. Briefly, the code says that it is essential that AOM members who consult "be guided by the ideals of *competence*, *integrity*, and *objectivity* (Italics ours)". This is accomplished through a variety of means, including representing credentials and capabilities accurately, fulfilling obligations in a responsible manner, maintaining confidentiality, negotiating clear and mutually accepted remuneration agreements and upholding "the legal and moral obligations of the society in which they function".

These ethical responsibilities are, of course, pertinent to any academic-practitioner relationship. They suggest that at the very least academics must be competent, honest and upfront, maintain confidentiality, and follow the law. It is within the context of these ethical obligations that this chapter is written.

2. Characteristics of practitioners on whom academics hope to be impacting and academics who might be better at connecting with them

As noted earlier, impact is often talked about generally, with some vague idea that it is addressed in particular to managers or at least in some position of influence, such as policymakers. (This may be especially the case in the UK, where recognition from a manager citing beneficial impact may be used to demonstrate impact.) There is no distinction made among types of practitioners who are being impacted.

However, as noted in Chapter 4, there are differences within the larger community of "practitioners", including the community of managers. Further, some managers are more likely to be open to academic work than others. To adopt a term often used in organisational change literature, some managers have more readiness for academic influence than others (Armenakis et al. 1993). In this section, we will focus on who is more likely to benefit from academic writing, reflection and collaboration and who is more likely to be able to provide these. Some practitioners are more open to this than others. Further, some academics may be better able to communicate with practitioners than others. Consider the following example.

McKenzie et al. (2014) conducted a study of participants in a Forum that engages academics and practitioners in exploratory research into issues associated with organisational learning. Among other things, they were interested in the types of sense-making that different participants engaged in at the Forum. They had been aware that there seemed to be some epistemological differences among participants and felt that it would be valuable to determine what was underneath these differences. In the course of their analysis, they learned that there were basically two sets of views of the Forum.

One of these was that the Forum could best be understood as a *partner in exploration* that plays largely a facilitative role, one that provides space for new thinking and learning with others. Forum members with this orientation were disposed to accept exploratory and explanatory activities at a conceptual level. The second view was that the Forum could best be understood as a *trusted advisor* that passed on knowledge that was immediately helpful. Those who held this view suggested priorities for community engagement that were pragmatic and emphasised the importance of re-enforcement of similar views along with a desire for practical tools that support immediate problem solving.

In other words, McKenzie et al. found that some of the participants in the forum made sense of what was going on in ways very similar to the academics; they were quite conceptually oriented. Others cared almost totally about how to apply learnings and hoped for very practical advice. In other words, some practitioners are more likely to find the conceptual dimensions of academic research stimulating, while others most definitely will not.

In addition, Donald Schön (1983) famously wrote about reflective practice in a way that is pertinent to academics and practitioners and that stops focusing on a rigour-relevance split. He said (p. 69) that: "The dilemma of rigor and relevance may be dissolved if we can develop an epistemology of practice which places technical problem solving within a broader context of reflexive inquiry, shows how reflection in action may be rigorous in its own right, and links the art of practice in uncertainty and uniqueness to the scientist's art of research. We may thereby increase the legitimacy of reflection in action and encourage its broader, deeper, and more rigorous use".

In other words, Schön's emphasis was on the ability for both academics and practitioners to be reflective. This is a quality that both may (or may not) share (cf. Crosina and Bartunek, 2017). It is likely that academics and practitioners who are reflective can share academic findings in a way that leads them both to share and develop ideas together.

A prime illustration of a scholar who can work with practice and is reflexive is Edgar Schein (Lambrechts et al., 2011: 132). Schein embodies scholarly practice, which can be understood as knowing "how to collaborate with practitioners in a joint inquiry and learning process aiming at formulating joint problem definitions and developing new and meaningful knowledge to the benefit of both academic and practitioner communities". There are other scholar-practitioners as well (cf. Empson, 2013; Wasserman and Kram, 2009), who also understand and appreciate both academia and practice.

What this discussion makes evident is that stereotypical distinctions between academics and practitioners do not entirely hold. There are ways members of the two communities are similar and members within each community differ from each other.

This may not appear to be an ethical issue in the sense in which such issues are usually discussed. However, it is definitely an issue of competence, which in turn is an ethical issue. It is a relational responsibility on the part of academics to attempt to be sensitive to the particular practitioners on whom one is hoping to have the type of impact discussed in Chapter 3. If nothing else, impact is more likely to be successful if it matches epistemologies.

3. The means through which impact takes place

Although these are not often discussed in formal discussions of impact, there are two important ways that impact takes place in practice. One of these is consulting (e.g. Butler et al., 2015) and the other is education (e.g. Anderson et al., 2017).

The role of consulting in conveying scholarly knowledge for practitioners has been contested for some time. For example, Kieser and Leiner (2009) pitted consultant knowledge against academic knowledge and suggested that consultants' less-academic knowledge is often more influential than academics' on practitioners.

However, in recent years, academics have more frequently done their own consulting (Butler et al., 2015; Marks et al., 2017) for reasons that go beyond commercial gain. This is indicated by the example of Schein earlier and is discussed more fully by Perkmann and Walsh (2008). The expectations of such academics are that consulting will be a "win-win" for both the academics and practitioners involved.

In fact, some scholar-practitioners consider consulting to be a primary way to further their research agenda. In this case, as Perkman and Walsh suggest, consulting is driven by the desire to understand more about a setting in which research might be used and to develop new research opportunities. However, there are often some ethical quandaries about this type of work, when, as Empson (2013) notes, engaging with organisations leads to some conflict with an academic scholarship. There are comparatively straightforward issues such as conflicts of interest and the needs to maintain anonymity, but there are also needs to clarify what knowledge is available for academic purposes and when.

Although this is not adequately considered, the primary means through which impact occurs is through education. Or, to put it better, in terms used in Chapters 2 and 3, one of the main places that scholarly research is performed and practice is influenced is in the classroom.

As Engwall and Kipping (2004: 243) note, business education is now a "dominant feature of many systems of higher education throughout the world". Thus, some concepts that are developed by academics are taught to students who (hopefully) implement them.

For example, the Black–Scholes options pricing model has been very influential for decades (Abrahamson et al., 2016). One of the reasons for its impact is that so many students learn how to use it in their economics classes (Bartunek, 2020). Something similar could be said about Michael Porter's (1980) five forces model. As Bartunek (p. 21) notes, this model "is taught to virtually every MBA student and undergraduate student taking a strategy class".

However, there are ethical issues here as well. Models such as these do not always fare well, as Lowenstein (2000) showed with the Black–Scholes model. Others (e.g. Fletcher, 2010) have described some questionable assumptions underlying the five forces model.

While these two models are particularly influential because of being learned in classes, they are not the only impactful approaches. In strategy classes and marketing classes, in particular, students are introduced to particular tools that they will put into practice (Wright et al., 2013), and there should be recognition of limits as well as strengths for such models.

Executive education is a particularly important source of impact. Tushman et al. (2007: 345), for example, argued that executive education "is an underutilized context that can enhance the quality of faculty research as well as our impact on managerial practice". This would be particularly the case "if executive education were more tightly coupled to managerial issues".

Ethical issues arise here as well. Büchel and Antunes (2007: 410), for example, emphasise that scholars engaged in executive education need "to develop the capacity not only to apply their own research to the organizational and individual context, but also to create research content that matters to practice". In other words, some academics are more suited to executive education than others, and choosing to become involved in this type of education represents an ethical choice. We develop the question of ethical quandaries associated with management education below.

4. Is academic training helpful or hurtful for managers and other practitioners?

As noted in Chapter 2, business schools have been subject to criticism when their alumni oversee the collapse or failure of institutions. The strongest questioning of whether academic training is helpful or hurtful was raised by Sumantra Ghoshal (2005), who famously argued that "bad management theories drive out good practice". His focus was on training in MBA classrooms.

Ghoshal argued "that academic research related to the conduct of business and management has had some very significant and negative influences on the practice of management. . . . I suggest that by propagating ideologically inspired amoral theories, business schools have actively freed their students from any sense of moral responsibility" (p. 76). He noted that, in contrast to much natural science, where how we think doesn't influence the behaviour of the materials under study, social science theories tend to be "self-fulfilling". That is, "a management theory-if it gains sufficient currency – changes the behaviors of managers who start acting in accordance with the theory" (p. 77). "Whether right or wrong to begin with, the theory can become right as managers – who are both its subjects and the consumers – adapt their behaviors to conform with the doctrine".

Ghoshal emphasised two specific problems. One was that a narrow use of positivist theories led to too narrow causal theories. This is problematic in particular because "the logic of falsification, which is so very essential for the epistemology of positivism, is very hard to apply with any degree of rigor and ruthlessness in the domain of social theories" (p. 87). The other is an ideology that focused on "solving the 'negative problem' of containing the costs of human imperfections" (p. 77). He focused in particular on agency theory, which "underlies the entire intellectual edifice in support of shareholder value maximization, (but) has little explanatory or predictive power".

Ghoshal argued that "the picture of the manager that emerges is one that is now very familiar in practice: the ruthlessly hard-driving, strictly top-down, command-and-control focused, shareholder-value-obsessed, win-at-any-cost business leader" (p. 85). This type of leadership led directly to many of the ethical lapses that were prevalent in the early 2000s. Further, Pfeffer (2005) noted that such training led MBA students to develop worse moral values over the sake of their training.

While Ghoshal focused on problems with MBA training, Kanter (2005: 83), in a response to his paper, asked "why has there been such a receptive audience? Why have these theories, and not others, been seized by consulting firms, policy makers, and others?" She suspected that "neoclassical 'economic man' theories seem to have more reach, resonance, and staying power than people-centered stakeholder relations theories. They are easier to teach, easier to do. Economic theories are neat. People are messy. Analytics are crisp, emotions are messy". Thus, Pfeffer argued that "The organizational studies and the education we do ought to, at least some of the time, engage with values".

In sum, this argument is that MBA faculty and industry leaders collude to teach values that are harmful, to treatment of employees and to ethical values more generally. The opportunity is available to management faculty to teach more positive values, along the lines emphasised by those at the University of Michigan developing "positive organization studies". However, many do not.

5. What is the expectation of types of impact?

In 1978, Pelz observed that "among writers about public policy, it has come to be axiomatic that social research in the United States has rarely been applied by public officials at any level" (p. 346). However, he went on to say that "this dismal picture may have arisen from an overly narrow definition of what is meant by social science knowledge and by 'utilization' of that knowledge" and that if we expand the understanding of utilisation "the use of social science knowledge may be more widespread than is generally supposed".

Thus, Pelz distinguished between instrumental, conceptual and symbolic uses of scholarship. He said that "The instrumental use of knowledge is equivalent to what has been called an 'engineering' or 'technical' or 'social-technological' function; the conceptual use of knowledge is equivalent to an 'enlightenment' function" (p. 350). He cited Weiss and Bucuvalas (1977: 226) who argue that "Research that challenges accepted ideas, arrangements, and programs obviously cannot be put to work in a direct and immediate way. It cannot be used instrumentally. . . . Yet, decision makers say it can contribute to their work and the work of other appropriate decision makers. It can enlighten them". He described a third type of use of scholarly knowledge as symbolic, such as when results of scholarship are used to legitimate a policy.

Several scholars (e.g. Beyer and Trice, 1982; Hamet and Maurer, 2017; Huber, 2018) have summarised Pelz's contribution. Beyer and Trice's (1982: 590) summary was illustrative, noting that (1) Instrumental use involves acting on research results in specific, direct ways. (2) Conceptual use involves using research results for general enlightenment; results influence actions, but in less specific, more indirect ways than in instrumental use. (3) Symbolic use involves using research results to legitimate and sustain pre-determined positions, for example, substituting the actions of the research process itself for other action, or using research results selectively or otherwise distorting them to justify actions taken for other reasons.

As Bartunek (2011: 18) noted, "Most discussions of the 'relevance' of management research implicitly, if not explicitly, seem to assume that the instrumental use of research findings is identical to relevance and thus despair when such work cannot be easily applied directly". However, there are clearly other contributions than that. Sometimes, in particular, providing conceptual stimulation is much more important than giving explicit directions regarding things to do.

However, regardless of whether the impact desired is instrumental or conceptual, it is important from the outset of a research project for there to be contact and collaboration between researchers and organisational members. Beyer (1997), for example, emphasised the necessity of contact between managers and scholars in conducting research, arguing that the methods used, and whether they involve direct contact with organisations, affect managers' confidence that the scholarly findings are based on true premises. This for her was an ethical issue. Rynes, McNatt & Bretz (1999) similarly found that how much time researchers spent at a research site early on affected how impactful a study became. Bartunek and Louis (1996) developed ways that external academics and insider members of an organisation can collaborate in scholarly research.

Thus, it is clear not only that the results of research may be used in multiple ways but also that how academics' immediate and personal contact with a research site affects its later impacts. As we suggest in Chapter 4, it is not enough simply to try to initiate one-time impact (of any kind) after a study is completed and published.

6. Complications of translation of academic writing for practice

One of the primary means of impact is through translation of academic articles for practitioners. This happens regularly through different types of news and social media. Many business schools publish scholarly magazines meant for practice. These include, among others, *Harvard Business Review*, *California Management Review*, *Warwick Core Insights* and *MIT Sloan Management Review*.

These news outlets are largely well received as helpful efforts, and there has been relatively little exploration of what such publication means from an ethical perspective. However, it has ethical components with respect to the role of translation of scholarly knowledge. This is not anywhere near as straightforward as it appears on the surface.

Because it is so common to translate medical research for patients, there is a considerable literature on this topic. Ren and Bartunek (2020) recently reviewed literature on the issues that have arisen in medical research related to this topic, to develop policies for management research. Their review uncovered a number of ethical issues associated with medical translation. One is that, as Bass (2016: 2334) commented, "lay people are yearning for information they can understand. They need explanations in plain language that fit their level of knowledge and anxiety, the chance to air options and risks with someone they can trust". In other words, translation of scholarly work by trustworthy people in medicine and, most likely in management, does matter.

Ren and Bartunek also noted that in translations in medical research the benefits of particular drugs are exaggerated, while the harm of such drugs is minimised. Similar things can happen in management translation when the emphasis is on the value of particular approaches (such as, say, Porter's five forces).

Further, as they noted, medical translators' work often encounters conflicting stakeholders. Knowledge translators of management research also face conflicting demands of original management research's need to be rigorous and accurate versus general reader's desire for interesting, sensational and prescriptive writing (Kelemen and Bansal, 2002).

Even more, potential readers may have conflicting interests with regard to new knowledge. This raises important questions: Who are the appropriate stakeholders and beneficiaries of academic research translation, and, thus, to whom are translators responsible? (p. 734). Are organisations and their top managers and/or, perhaps, lower-level employees supposed to benefit? Is society at large supposed to benefit? Is there competition between stakeholders in such a way that what benefits one set of stakeholders may harm others? For example, if managers learn effective ways of firing an employee, does that mean they are more likely to do so?

Of course, translators may have little control over how the findings will actually be used, especially symbolically. For example, the large amount of gender research that shows how women are generally underpaid, presented lower offers than their male counterparts request smaller compensations or achieve lower results than males in negotiations (e.g. Ayres, 1991; Blau and

Kahn, 2007) can be cited by gender equality advocates as supporting their positions but can at the same time be used to (covertly) support organisations continuing to make lower offers to women. It is at least important for knowledge translators to recognise these possibilities.

Of course, in terms of language, management is quite different from hard science disciplines such as physics, medicine and chemistry. While lay readers may find research papers in physics/medicine/chemistry full of impenetrable words, we may be able to recognise most of the words used in a management research paper. However, this does not necessarily make translation easier.

7. Whether impact should be thought of only as one directional from academics to practitioners

The implicit assumption is typically that academics have impacts on practitioners. However, that is unlikely to be adequate as an expectation. As noted earlier by Kanter (2005), for example, practitioners often have impacts on academics, such as providing demand for particular types of academic knowledge.

Practitioner approaches can also stimulate academic thinking. A major illustration was found in a paper by Barley, Meyer and Gash (1984) that explored the comparative extent to which academics' definition of culture had an impact on practitioners' definitions and vice versa. They found that practitioners' definitions, which tended to emphasise values, had more impacts on academics' interpretations of culture than academics' had on practitioners. In addition, books such as Peters' and Waterman's (1982) *In Search of Excellence* and Peter Senge's (1990) *The Fifth Discipline* have had major impacts on academic thinking. Many academics use the term "mental models" without awareness of that it came from Senge's work.

Ployhart and Bartunek (2019: 496) argued that "practitioner-based insights are especially needed in a world that is increasingly volatile, uncertain, and complex. If scholars are to develop theory that influences practically relevant research in a timely manner, then tight connections to practitioners are vital for ensuring that theory is grounded in phenomena and meaningful organizational problems". This is consistent with the approach presented earlier, that academics' close involvement with practice is very helpful for their scholarship's long-term impact. It is also helpful for addressing issues that are most salient to (at least some) practitioners.

8. On what topics should academics strive to have impact?

As noted earlier, the British Academy of Management statement of values emphases that BAM aims "to be inclusive, recognise and respect the diversity in our community". It adds that "BAM sets out to Provide a welcoming, supportive pluralistic community of scholarship".

The Academy of Management ethical code adds that "members also have a responsibility to all people with whom we live and work in the world community. Sensitivity to other people, to diverse cultures, to the needs of the poor and disadvantaged, to ethical issues, and to newly emerging ethical dilemmas is required. . . . Further, in their role as educators, members of the Academy can play a vital role in encouraging a broader horizon for decision making by viewing issues from a multiplicity of perspectives, including the perspectives of those who are the least advantaged".

These statements mean that BAM and AOM members are expected to be knowledgeable about broader societal concerns, not only those of managers. Further, they should be able to view issues from multiple perspectives (as suggested in Chapter 3). This is very different from telling people one perspective or one thing to do. Rather, the expectation is that the work that Academics do will matter in the larger world. This kind of emphasis is mirrored activities such as Anne Tsui's Network that addresses Responsible research in Business and Management, www.rrbm.network/. It is also embodied in work that Andrew Hoffman and his colleagues do at the ERB Institute at the University of Michigan, https://erb.umich.edu/, the work of Tima Bansal and the Network for Business Sustainability at Western University, www.nbs.net/, the Rotterdam School of Management's emphasis on the UN's sustainable development goals, www.rsm.nl/sustainability/sustainable-rsm-positive-change/, the centre for effective organisations partnering with other universities and with practitioner partners from multiple countries to conduct research and design work for sustainable effectiveness (Mohrman, 2018) and many more examples. The great majority of these efforts involve practitioners and academics working together in ventures in which the knowledge of both is necessary to address issues adequately (cf. Crosina and Bartunek, 2017).

In the spring of 2020, Edgar Schein now in his nineties, but still very concerned about our work, wrote what he labelled a "rant":

> The next pandemic will be global warming and the collapse of pieces of the global environment. We already see early symptoms with the heat waves, the floods, the uncontrollable wildfires, hurricanes and other weather changes. At the same time, the virus pandemic has revealed how much our environment is capable of cleaning itself if we give it a fighting chance. Can we take advantage of what we observe globally as the positive impact of our staying home for a couple of months?
>
> The current virus pandemic will force some shift from *rampant competition* among countries, states, hospital units, and systems based on

economic well-being rather than global health, to inventing processes of *collaboration* that protect the common resources pertaining to world health.

Will we recognize that we need to use or invent methods of *collaboration* on a global level to deal with the global environment as a finite resource that we are currently depleting by encouraging or at least sanctioning *rampant competition* among countries, industries, and political parties?

Social scientists have found many examples of how *collaboration* is necessary to avoid the tragedy of the commons, the unwitting depletion of limited resources. Can we now put forth what we know and what we believe in to escalate *collaboration* as a central value in ameliorating the inevitable next global pandemic around global warming?

This is clearly a call for the importance of academics, together with skilled practitioners, addressing global issues that really matter in the world. It, along with some examples earlier, recognises that what we address is very important in itself, and it is an ethical responsibility for us to respond.

9. Some challenges of impact

Finally, we will consider some potential challenges of impact that often are not acknowledged. One major challenge is of being in the public sphere, debating one's position with others (Etzion and Gehman, 2019). A position may be more or less popular but it will surely evoke strong feelings from those who disagree with it.

If our scholarship is to have the impact that some other scholarship such as medicine does, we must be prepared for a much stronger and more negative response to us than is the case now. For example, at the time of this writing, Dr. Anthony Fauci is the director of the National Institute of Allergy and Infectious Diseases in the US, a position that is particularly important, due to the COVID-19 virus. One of his roles is to tell Americans what to do to lessen the impact of the virus. However, this is not always taken well by Americans either who do not believe the virus is real or who do not want anyone encroaching on their freedom. As a result, Dr. Fauci received death threats and his adult daughters were harassed (www.npr.org/sections/coronavirus-live-updates/2020/08/05/899415906/fauci-reveals-he-has-received-death-threats-and-his-daughters-have-been-harassed). This is not something that management scholars tend to think about as one of the outcomes of impact. It clearly has ethical implications.

Conclusion

In conclusion, there are multiple ethical issues intertwined with impact, many more than most would imagine. They typically do not venture into legal issues. However, they do make evident that impact can be much more complicated than is usually acknowledged. These ethical complications serve to make evident how important impact can be.

Notes

1 www.bam.ac.uk/about-bam/about-bam.html
2 https://aom.org/About-AOM/AOM-Code-of-Ethics.aspx

6 Nurturing the capacity to create impact

In this book, we addressed the issue of impact in management research. Specifically, we have considered how, when and for whom management research creates impact and what forms that impact takes. Achieving impact sounds as though it should be relatively straightforward, at least in being able to assess whether or not academic ideas have changed management practice. However, when we explore what actually happens empirically it is clear that simple causal relations rarely, if ever, play out. In contrast to the linear, logical and academically led view of impact embedded in much of what informs current thinking on impact, our exposition in this book suggests a dynamic interaction of roles, skills, purposes, techniques, practices and cultural contexts. Therefore, we have proposed a model of impact that is processual, contextual and that incorporates different impact types that enable the actors to make choices about how they proceed. Impact is processual in that it takes place over time and is often iterative as ideas and practices are experimented with and reflected upon (see Figure 2, Chapter 1). It is contextual in that changes are embedded in immediate environments of application and in meta-level learning that develops from the immediate action to theoretical and methodological innovations for academics and further re-applications of the practice into new contexts for managers (see Figure 1, Chapter 1). Actors bring different skills to the collaborative venture of creating impact, such as analytical skills, technical skills, political and practical skills as well as skills in translation and translocution (cf. Palo et al., 2020). Creating impact is very much a "team sport" since it is unlikely that any individual could possess all these skills at a sufficient level. Further, such skills are constituents of learning where learning itself incorporates reflexivity and praxis as a meta-concept that draws together the diverse practices and theories we have considered in this book. Learning as a form of enquiry enables the interplay of practice and theory that lie at the heart of impact and of achieving observable change. Therefore, in this concluding chapter, we consider the role that management academics can play in connecting disciplines and areas of professional practice and the skills required to achieve. We also consider the cultural context which places emphasis and significance on the achievements of some above others. If we accept the basic premise of impact as a team sport, it follows that we need to understand the restrictions and permissible spheres of action that academics and professionals operate within and the consequent demands of performativity, and some would say hegemony.

In conceptualising impact in this interconnected and imbricated way, we realise that there may be clashes with organisational and institutional expectations of impact, which assume a singularity of causation such as through assessing impact based on counting measures such as through altmetrics. We also realise that our perspective has implications for the ways in which academics develop their careers, give attention to skills development and nurture their own reflexive practice.

In this chapter, we return to a theme from Chapter 2 as we consider in more detail the ways in which a particular institutionalised conceptualisation of impact, introduced from outside of the individual's and Higher Education Institution's (HEI's) control, can begin to perform a particular version of impact praxis. We consider the tensions with current academic practice that such performances can generate. We compare the tensions between traditional research publishing and emerging impact praxis that are being built bottom-up from engaged research projects that are complex, interdisciplinary and longitudinal and explore how they might be reconciled. Finally, we consider what it means for academics on the front line, their skills development and key choices they make at critical career junctures.

Performing specific impact conceptualisation and artefacts

In Chapter 3, we discussed the performative nature of theory and the role of *theory in use* in developing both impact and theory. It is useful to extend these ideas to the role that particular conceptualisation of impact play in shaping how impact is performed in practice, along with the institutional devices that capture and represent such conceptualisations and are designed to shape such practices. Such institutional devices might include strategic objectives set by HEIs, the specification of performance criteria required for promotion or career advancement. But, importantly, they can include performance frameworks that come from outside of the HEIs themselves, such as the UK's "Research Excellence Framework" (REF), which grades the research "Outputs", "Environment" and "Impact Case Studies" of a particular HEI.

Here we will explore, in more detail, the REF impact framework introduced in Chapter 2 and provide an illustration of how such devices configure so many management research lives and so shape what many do as researchers, and our understandings of the skills they need to develop. It is not our intention here to use the REF impact framework as an exemplar. Rather, we use it to show how institutions and research environments shape how academics perform impact. Being aware how conceptualisation of impactful research shapes our actions is as important to managers of research in HEIs as it is to individual researchers, practitioners and policymakers.

REF is one of the most established frameworks for evaluating research at national level and has taken place every 4–7 years since 1992 in the UK. Over time, other countries have developed equivalent frameworks in including, for example, ERA (Excellence in Research for Australia) and PBRF (New Zealand's Performance-Based Research Framework). Whilst the particularities of the UK REF exercise do not apply everywhere, it nevertheless serves as a useful basis on which to examine the ways in which attempts to measure impact, themselves have impact.

In the REF2021 framework, which is forthcoming as this book is being written, business and management research is submitted to a panel specifically for "Business and Management" research evaluation. "Guidance on Submission" and "Panel Criteria and Working Methods" are published by Research England, the government agency responsible for administering the REF evaluation process. The outcome of the evaluation determines the monies distributed to each HEI by government for the following period; higher-performing HEIs get more "QR" (Quality Research) money. This is an important stream of income for HEIs. Equally, if not more importantly, the REF plays a significant role in establishing status differentials between individual academic schools and indeed whole universities. Although not intended for this purpose, it is used in journalistic league tables (see e.g. the Times Higher Education (THE) "Best Universities" guide and the Forbes "Top Colleges" guide), which produce an easily classifiable, consumable version of universities arranged in a hierarchy. Position in the hierarchy influences market position, influence with policymakers and the ability to attract staff. Consequently, the REF framework performs new realities, shaping strategy, policy and practices across HEIs, from the organisational to the individual level. REF documents are, therefore, performative in the development of research programmes, the strategic investments universities make and the representation of researchers' activities within specific REF templates.

The REF2021 documents "Guidance on Submission"[1] and "Panel Criteria and Working Methods"[2] the *Impact Case Studies* template together provide a specific conceptualisation of research impact. The guidance defines impact in a very specific way. First, by laying out the parameters of what qualifies as impact in relation to research quality and time. Guidance specifies that the research underpinning the impact being claimed must be judged to be at quality level "2" (with level 4 being the highest quality), "Quality that is recognised internationally in terms of originality, significance and rigour". Time parameters are presented thus: "Case studies describing specific examples of impacts achieved during the assessment period (1 August 2013 to 31 July 2020), underpinned by research in the period 1 January 2000 to 31 December 2020)" (p. 1, Guidance on Submission). From the standpoint of anyone seeking to assess impact it is perhaps understandable to time-bound submissions. The practical merit of this is to have dates, before which or after which, evidence of impact is regarded as inadmissible. The perhaps unintended consequence is, however, to artificially regiment the kind of multi-actor, relational, diffuse and temporally dispersed form of impact that we have argued for in this book.

Second, the Guidance lays out assessment criteria, "The sub-panels will assess the 'reach and significance' of impacts on the economy, society, culture, public policy or services, health, the environment or quality of life [beyond academia] that were underpinned by excellent research conducted in the submitted unit" (p. 7, Guidance on Submission). The terms "reach and significance" are important evaluation criteria:

> 288. **Reach** will be understood as the extent and/or diversity of the beneficiaries of the impact, as relevant to the nature of the impact. Reach will be assessed in terms of the extent to which the potential constituencies, number of groups of beneficiaries have been reached; it will not be assessed in purely geographic terms, nor in terms of absolute number of beneficiaries. The criteria will be applied wherever the impact occurred, regardless of geography or location, and whether in the UK or abroad.
>
> 289. **Significance** will be understood as the degree to which the impact has enabled, enriched, influenced, informed or changed the performance, policies, practices, products, services, understanding, awareness or wellbeing of the beneficiaries.
>
> (p. 52, Panel Criteria and Working Methods)

The guidance also states that the panel will make an overall judgement about the reach and significance of impacts, rather than assessing them as separate criteria. It provides examples of impact:

> 298. Impact includes, but is not limited to, an effect, change or benefit to:
>
> • The activity, attitude, awareness, behaviour, capacity, opportunity, performance, policy, practice, process or understanding.

- Of an audience, beneficiary, community, constituency, organisation or individuals.
- In any geographic location whether locally, regionally, nationally or internationally.

299. Impact includes the reduction or prevention of harm, risk, cost or other negative effects.

(p. 68, Guidance on Submission)

And provides a rating table of definitions for their application (see Table 6.1):

Finally, the Guidance provides a template for the presentation of Impact Case Studies, with a prescription of typeface, margins, spacing and maximum number of pages (five pages) for the presentation of each case (Appendix 6.1). We are aware that REF is one specific incidence of an assessment framework that pertains only to the UK. We have already noted that some other countries have developed similar approaches whilst other countries feature no assessment at all. However, we would contend that at the level of the individual HEI, there is a growing awareness of, and narrative around, the need to make a difference, and the REF is much more specific about what this means than do other measures, which generally emphasise civic mission, closeness to industry or a similar sense of relevance. Thus, we suggest that even academics operating in an environment where there is no national assessment framework for impact should pay close attention to the ways in which impactfulness is accounted for both in their own institution and in their own story of self. Returning to the UK example of REF with this caveat in mind, it is easy to see how any such framework may be used

Table 6.1 REF2021 published criteria for assessing impacts

The criteria for assessing impact are "reach" and "significance":

- In assessing the impact described within a case study, the panel will form an overall view about its "reach and significance" taken as a whole, rather than assess "reach and significance" separately.

Four star	Outstanding impacts in terms of their reach and significance.
Three star	Very considerable impacts in terms of their reach and significance.
Two star	Considerable impacts in terms of their reach and significance.
One star	Recognised but modest impacts in terms of their reach and significance.
Unclassified	The impact is of little or no reach and significance; or the impact was not eligible; or the impact was not underpinned by excellent research produced by the submitted unit.

to judge researcher as impactful or not and, therefore, through time, begins to reconfigure engaged research praxis.

Emerging tensions within academic practices

Our observations suggest that REF2021 impact criteria are configuring specific types of investments in the research process and are directing researchers to fundamentally different and often opposing practices, than, say a researcher aiming solely to publish in a leading academic journal. For example, the REF2021 conceptualisations of impact – the need to bring about real change in the world and the need to measure and evidence that change – require considerable resources, significant amounts of research funding and interdisciplinary teams of researchers working collaboratively with research partners such as companies, NGOs and government agencies. The development of "pathways to impact" that includes, for example, new practitioner education programmes, engagement events and/or design and delivery "sprints", as outlined in Chapters 2 and 3, often become a core component of grant applications, and requires professional support to enable their delivery. Further, the investment in collecting, collating and assembling accessible and meaningful bundles of corroborating evidence to support REF2021 impact case studies is considerable. The REF2021 definition of impact has resulted in some HEIs creating new roles for professional service personnel whose sole task is to collect evidence of impact. The impact definition has also resulted in the development of incentive and reward schemes that encourage researchers to engage with key stakeholder communities to try and drive change based on their emerging or developed theorisation of their research findings.

One particular characteristic of the REF2021 conceptualisation of impact is the time period within which both the underpinning research [and theoretical development] and the impact [changes brought about by those specific theoretical developments] have to be attributed to the HEI. This means both bodies of research and impact activity need to be firmly anchored within a specific HEI (rather than being solely attached to individual researchers) which, understandably, has consequences for the motivations of those reporting the impact and the nature of those impacts, hidden from public view because they don't "count", and which might not be reported. Accounting for impact in this way requires significant investments. The establishment of *all university* interdisciplinary research centres and institutes is an example of such an investment. The recruitment of early career researchers with the specific purpose of transforming them into cereal large grant award winners is another. Configured by these impact case requirements, coupled with the changing requirements of the government agencies responsible for making competitive research grant awards, the emphasis on the need for significant scale and scope of impact is now clear in the UK and becoming more of a priority in other countries.

This performative conceptualisation of REF2021 impact marks a move away from the small study, top publication, lone or paired researcher models that have sustained our business and management schools over the past decade, and towards large, long-term efforts focused on impact, societal and economic improvements. Supported by interdisciplinary and multi-skilled professional support staff, the new aim of the UK Universities at least is to foster inquiry into real-world solutions for complex and perplexing problems over sustained periods of time (typically 3–10 years). This is changing the way Deans are thinking about the recruitment and staffing mix of their Business and Management Schools, the promotion criteria and pluralisation of career paths, and ultimately, it is beginning to change the way individual researchers understand, make sense of and perform their individual research roles and careers.

The changes for researchers are potentially significant. In the UK context, successive national assessment exercises have heightened the focus on publishing research in highly ranked journals. This has meant that many researchers work alone or in small groups of two or three, frame their research projects around particular theoretical problems and within the specific onto-epistemological traditions of the "top" journals. Researchers spend years heavily investing in developing academic networks, learning the language game of those networks (Wittgenstein, 1953; Beech, 2008) and learning how to develop their argumentation, craft papers and the representation of evidence in specific ways to publish in a small number of journals within a specific field. As we explained in Chapters 1 and 3, these practices have resulted in concerns and explicit criticisms about the divorcing of rigour from relevance in the business and management journals, in a way that other disciplines have not encountered (cf. Mason et al., 2015). In several places in this book, we have also discussed the nature of management as pluralistic and so difficult to define and characterise as a profession (specifically, see Chapter 2). Together, management research requirements and management "profession" characteristics can appear to conspire to prevent business and management researchers from grounding the framing of their research in practical problems. Specialist reviewer communities struggle to review and recognise quality interdisciplinary research framed in this way or value practical insight and explanation. In the past, HEIs have incentivised and rewarded publishing and small group collaboration management research practices and outcomes, with academic publication ideals driving Business and Management School recruitment, career progression and practice. Today, however, the landscape is changing.

In addition, many international HEIs are now signed up to the San Francisco Declaration of Research Assessment (https://sfdora.org/) which commits individuals and HEIs to evaluating research outputs in their own right and *not* based on the use of journal impact factors, journal rankings or over reliance of citations. This change, together with the growing significance of the impact agenda (MacIntosh et al., 2017), is changing the skills that researchers need.

Our observations here are not that these changes will eradicate the value of publishing in "top" journals but rather that researchers and HEIs are having to rethink, redefine and expand the characteristics of what constitutes "good research", including its performance and outputs. These changes will have important consequences for the performance of individual's research practices.

The aim of business and management researchers, as a result of this changing research landscape, is to create a virtuous circle between quality engagement that attracts and speaks to research funding agency agenda in a useful and valuable way, that then enables the collection and analysis of high-quality data and that provides the materials for high-quality outputs (for policy, practitioners *and* researchers communities), which in turn drive and open-up further valuable engagements, engaged research and impact (Figure 6.1).

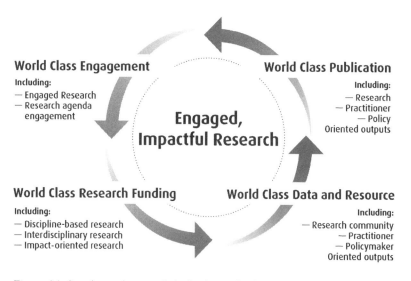

Figure 6.1 Creating a virtuous circle for the production of impactful research

Forums for fostering engaged research and impact

Centres fostering impact. Several collaborative research centres have been established to facilitate such virtuous circles for impactful research and aimed at developing impact praxis bottom-up. A few examples include the Impact Scholar Community, the Strategy Scholars Network, the Open Innovation Team within the UK Government's Cabinet Office and the Behavioral Science and Policy Association.

The Impact Scholar Community[3] is an international online community of organisational scholars and educators conducting research to solve real-world problems. It defines impact as evident when (1) our research changes how organisations and decision makers think and act and (2) we use our position as academics to foster positive change beyond our immediate research insights. This community is sponsored by the Organisations and the Natural Environment division of the Academy of Management, though potential contributions go beyond environmental issues.

The Scholars Strategy Network[4] is a US-based organisation of university-based scholars who are committed to using research to improve policy and strengthen democracy across the states. As it says on its website, the Scholars Strategy Network is working to advance the use of research wherever policy decisions are made – from city halls to state legislatures to Washington.

Scholars have also worked with policymaking officials in the UK to create the Open Innovation Team practitioners within the UK Government's Cabin Office, Whitehall; generating a permanent structure designed to facilitate just such engagements across multiple and complex policymaking initiatives so that academics from different disciplines and policymakers can jointly explore and co-produce policy.[5] This initiative is now being led by policymakers rather than scholars, and brings researchers into projects from across the world, as and when expertise is needed.

The Behavioral Science and Policy Association[6] describes itself as "a global community of public and private sector decision makers, behavioral science researchers, policy analysts, and practitioners with a bold mission to promote the application of rigorous behavioral science research that serve the public interest. We serve as an information hub, and community builder-connecting individuals and organizations through our conferences, spotlight workshops, taskforces, and the publication of newsletters and behavioral science & policy". These organising structures act as valuable catalysers of research projects.

One particularly useful example of a university-based collaborative projects is the Global Challenge Research Funded "RECIRCULATE" project, led by Lancaster University, UK (http://wp.lancs.ac.uk/recirculate/).

"RECIRCULATE" is delivering a solution-focused research project that sets out to deliver innovative solutions to pressing problems concerning water use and safety through entrepreneurial activity, in Africa. RECIRCULATE is working to "join up" the different ways in which water sustains communities from sewage disposal to energy generation and water used in food production. The aim is to provide people with a good living from caring for and using water well. Part of RECIRCULATE's ambition is being realised collaboratively through a second project, spawned by RECIRCULATE, call ACTUATE, (http://imagination.lancaster.ac.uk/project/actuate/). The ACTUATE project, working with partners to develop an anaerobic digestion demonstrator system in Ghana and Nigeria to deliver electricity, sanitation improvements and sustainable fertiliser for crops share partners and researchers with RECIRCULATE.

Both RECIRCULATE and ACTUATE are based on an interdisciplinary co-designed research approach. Solving these types of complex, real-world research problems demands the use of the new collaborative approaches outlined in this book. In RECIRCULATE's case, researchers are concerned with how European-born research is resituated and translated to meet the needs of communities across Africa, making it generative of management and other research as a project in its own right. In other words, the resituating of theories – as described in Chapters 3 and 4 – in Africa transforms the management work into more than an "implementation science" but through the collaboration with local experts is generative of new research insights and findings; theories of entrepreneurship, business networks and inter-organisational relationships are transformed.

As discussed in Chapter 5, these types of projects have deep ethical implications connected with how researchers make themselves aware of local needs, the knowledge and experience of their collaborators and partners and for how these collaborations are performed and unfolded. (For a sobering example of an unethical approach to such impact see Whiteman and Cooper (2016)). By combining excellence in scientific research (environmental science, crop science, engineering and microbiology), social science and management research (entrepreneurial learning and knowledge exchange), across partners and disciplines, and working with business and other research users, these projects are co-designing research to deliver appropriate solution *with* African partners. The point here is that researchers, practitioners and policymakers are building cutting-edge solutions to addressing the global challenges around safe and sustainable water use *together*. This project includes a substantial training element, focused training events in Africa and 4–8 weeks "residences" at Lancaster University, using Lancaster's award-winning model of eco-innovation where academics and research students work with business.

The RECIRCULATE project is born out of the Centre for Global Eco-Innovation, established in 2012 as a multi-partner Centre led by Lancaster University, aimed at delivering sustainable and equitable societies and economies, including sustainable development. It was conceptualised from the outset as a route to delivering the "green economy", which the World Bank estimated in 2015, had a global value of $3.4 trillion and is predicted to grow to more than $8 trillion by 2025. Through the structured support of the Centre, RECIRCULATE is delivering innovative products, toolkits and services that are providing new business opportunities for local entrepreneurs; is achieving more efficient and responsible use of natural resources; is reducing impact on the environment, including contributing to a low carbon economy in all sectors; and is enhancing societal, economic and technological resilience to environmental pressures. Policymakers at local, national and pan-African levels have expressed their strong support for this ethical, collaborative mode of working as a route to supporting green growth and climate change adaptation across the continent.

What has been interesting in this project has been the impact at multiple levels. In Chapter 1, these were identified as level 1, the initial project level, impacting the communities and stakeholders at hand and generating value in the immediate setting; at a meta level, the broader social, economic or technical level, where groups beyond the immediate project partners are enrolled and impacted; and for academics, where the methodological and process impacts engage researchers in reflexive practices regarding how they work with partners and other researchers. In conversation, researchers have reported to us how they have been changed by their research projects, reframing their research questions, exploring new theoretical perspectives as a result of their practical, engaged research experiences with collaborators and seeking new forms of collaboration with different kinds of collaborators, in new places and spaces. On the RECIRCULATE project that they had "seen entrepreneurship in a completely new light – not recognised in the literature at all". In each project, researchers gave accounts of how difficult it was to follow the traces of the impact of their work, how difficult it was to directly attribute it to specific actions they and their collaborators had been involved with and how impact often carried on, far beyond the boundaries of the project and their line of sight. In other words, they understood and gave meaning to them through action, not post action. They too saw impact as messy, non-linear and grounded in collaborative relations.

Impact praxis and skills development

An important reflection is that in many cases, and certainly in the two research projects outlined earlier, researchers developed new skills as a direct result of being involved in large, interdisciplinary research projects. Table 6.2 identifies the skills we have observed as being developed through such complex projects, by academics, at different career stages. Many of these skills relate directly to the four forms of impact outlined in Chapter 1. At the early career stage, researchers are developing their knowledge, quality research, publication and communication skills. To develop their impact skills, researchers are often learning to engage with non-academic audiences and using pro-active engagement with research participants and potential other stakeholders to help them think about their research questions and agenda through the use of theory to engage in dialogic interactions (as described in Chapter 4) and translocutions (as described in Chapter 3; Palo et al., 2020). These activities and skills appear to be what is enabling early career researchers to become more reflexive, helping them to reframe what matters theoretically *and* practically and helping them to more easily uncover what is difficult or unknown and why in both practical and theoretical communities.

At the end of the research process, early career researchers are more engaged with communicating findings to broader audiences through presentations and through practitioner-facing outlets which often feature a different editorial process quite different from that of blind, peer review. In Chapter 5, we discussed the ethical challenges that researchers face when working to make their work accessible to non-academic audiences and it seems pertinent that we should do more to help early career researchers take these steps and be more prepared for the challenges of implications of doing this difficult work well. Examples of platforms that support non-academic communication of research findings include business and management school magazines, learned society sponsored forums such as AOM Insights (https://journals.aom.org/journal/amiI) and *The Conversation* – which is a network of not-for-profit media outlets that publish copyright-free news stories on the Internet that are written by academics and researchers. Such platforms can have significant reach. For example, publishing all content under a Creative Commons license, *The Conversation* reports a monthly online audience of 10.7 million users onsite and a combined reach of 40 million people including republication (Dickinson, 2016).

The key learning for researchers when engaging with these platforms is that they often enrol academics in working with journalists who help them learn how to communicate complex theories and findings in an accessible way. This kind of work is an explicit expectation of the Impact Scholar Community, which provides support to young scholars in working with journalists. Such channels are not exclusive to early career researchers of course, but learning to engage throughout the research process, including in the communication of findings, often represents the first stage of impact skills development for researchers. In other words, at the early career researcher stage, the primary focus is on the development of research and communication skills. It is perhaps not surprising then that it is Type One (theories that influence academic practice) and Two impacts (models and frameworks that orient the direction of good practice) that are more typically produced at this career stage (see Figure 1, Chapter 1).

Promotion criteria vary both by geography and by institution type. In most institutions, researchers at mid-career levels have typically already had to demonstrate an aptitude for publishing and in more research-intensive settings that publishing experience will focus on top-ranked academic journals. Mid-career, the emphasis begins to shift from proving that one can publish, to publishing in sufficient volumes and in the "right" destinations to reach the highest attainable role (e.g. full professor, tenure) whilst beginning to consolidate knowledge and experience such that individual scholars can engage with much broader academic audiences – increasingly in interdisciplinary settings through their engagement with research centres or institutes in their own or other HEIs, nationally and internationally. Mid-Career is where, in the UK at least and in some European countries, we see the greatest potential for impact skills development and for significant progress to be made with opportunities for researchers to "step out of the publishing rat race", by taking time to develop interdisciplinary and increasingly engaged methods of researching that are explicitly designed to bring about positive, impactful change. In the US, many HEIs don't expect a high level of engaged research and impact, though it tends to be more emphasised after scholars have become full professors, at which point, generally, scholars have more freedom to follow their interest in impactful research in this broader sense.

At more senior stages, management researchers may become Co-investigators or Principle Investigators on large grants[7] for the first time. Such experiences require management researchers to learn how to design-in impact for research projects, often as a requirement of the grant as described in Chapters 2 and 3; to learn how to engage in dialogue with different publics, policymakers and practitioners (Chapter 4), so that they become partners in both the development and delivery of the research and the change it is designed to promote and implement. This has implications for skills development in leading impact initiatives and acting ethically and reflexively (Chapters 4 and 5) both as part of the research project and beyond. The aim here is to ensure that engagement and collaboration do simulate new ways of seeing and understanding the world, and to reshape research agendas, so removing the rigour-relevance critique raised in Chapters 2 and 3. Another key skill associated with the design and delivery of these types of complex, multidisciplinary, multi-stakeholder projects are impact evidencing skills: qualifying, quantifying and valuing positive change. This means developing skills that enable researchers to both value and evaluate impact activities and outcomes, enabling them to demonstrate, for example, reach and significance at local, regional, national and international scales. This is important not just because of quality assessment exercises such as REF but because such approaches will enable our research community to know what works, generating better performative evaluation of promising practices that can be developed and adapted as they are resituated and reused (Mason et al., 2019; Palo et al., 2020). As we have highlighted, leading, participating and delivering parts of such complex projects are often transformative experiences for researchers; transforming their framing of research problems, their presentation of argument and actionable change and even their methodological approaches to research. Such efforts have the potential to deliver all four impact types, including Type Three, methods for impactful research where the reflexivity of the researchers with practitioners lead to the further development of a new praxis of methods and, Type Four, where the reflexivity of practitioners with researcher leads to the production of practice examples, guidance and changes in praxis.

Later-career academics, with established research reputations of international standing, will likely develop and draw on their leadership experience and lead complex real-world research projects and centres of research excellence. They need to develop the skills that enable them to establish their reputation with external non-academic bodies, NGOs and organisations and to continue developing their knowledge of broader societal concerns. They also need to develop skills relating to evidence the reach and significance of research impact, in relation to their work and in relation to the work of their collaborators. At this career stage, non-academic outputs seem to be very impactful and learning how to produce and disseminate work that is accessible and informs policy development and positive change in organisational practice. Long-term, longitudinal relationships are also of significant research value at this career stage, both for the individual and their HEI. Again, at this career stage, all four forms of impact should be achievable and desirable, though extensive experience may mean that Type Three (new methods for impactful research) may be less dynamic at this career stage.

The role of business and management researchers in complex, interdisciplinary impactful research projects

To conclude, we reflect on the interesting lessons relevant to generating impactful research in relation to understanding context, the performativity of theory in use, dialogic interaction and ethical praxis. We do so, to better understand what we can all do to become more impactful researchers in

Table 6.2 Skill development for impactful research

Focus	Skills development		
	Early career	Mid career	Later career
Impact on scholarship	• Understand and communicate field relevant advances in knowledge in own field; • Learn to conduct high-quality research; • Learn to publish quality research outputs of international excellence; • Learn to produce competitive applications for small external funding.	• Develop expert knowledge of multiple themes and methods in related disciplinary areas and understanding of practical implications; • Learn to communicate core ideas to relevant academic audiences outside of the discipline; • Learn to listen and identify connections between your own work and that from other disciplines outside of business and management; • Learn to develop intradisciplinary and interdisciplinary networks; • Learn to engage and take on leadership roles in interdisciplinary research centres and institutes; • Learn to supervise doctoral researchers so that they develop disciplinary expertise but are aware of interdisciplinary research and its relevance to their agenda.	• Establish and grow research reputation of international standing; • Learn to develop and deliver research strategy; • Leading large, interdisciplinary grant writing and delivery projects; • Leading research centres, institutes and/or networks; • Managing and delivering a high-quality research outputs pipeline; • Sustain a record of doctoral research supervision; • Actively engage in and lead all university and inter-university research projects.

(Continued)

Table 6.2 (Continued)

Focus	Skills development		
	Early career	*Mid career*	*Later career*
Impact on practice	• Learn to become pro-active in engaging non-academic actors to shape your individual research agenda; • Learn the ethic of engagement, collaboration and translation; • Learn to become pro-active in communicating research findings with non-academic audiences.	• Learn to design-in impact to research projects; • Learn to engage in dialogue with publics, policymakers and practitioners; • Learn to lead impact initiatives; • Learn to establish and manage engagement relationships relevant to your research agenda; • Learn to evaluate and demonstrate the reach and significance of research locally, regionally, nationally and internationally; • Learn to work with professional support staff to identify opportunities for and extend the reach of impact.	• Establish reputation with external non-academic bodies and clients; • Evidence reach and significance of research impact in relation to your own work and with your collaborators and co-workers; • Learn to produce work that informs policy development and/or positive change in policy and organisational practice; • Learn to lead and secure productive, high-impact partnerships with business, policymakers and other users of our research expertise with evidence of significant income generation.

our complex, interdisciplinary and multi-stakeholder research project roles. The collaboration and coordination of such engaged, multi-stakeholder research projects and the integration and value of management, market and organisational studies to projects that, at first sight, appear to be about solving technical problems, is worthy of note. In both the complex real-world projects presented in this chapter, interdisciplinary, engaged research put management at the forefront, not only for organising the development and implementation of new and transformed socio-technical system but also, additionally, for the skills and knowledge management scholars bring to managing the complexities of the projects themselves.

We identify five key illustrations of praxis that researchers, their collaborators and partners can adopt to develop themselves as impactful researchers and collaborators in this new landscape of large grants, and complex, real-world interdisciplinary research projects designed to support the development and implementation of impactful research and bring about sustained, real-world change for the common good.

1   Develop contemporary understandings of socio-economic concerns. All actors – researchers from all disciplines, business, NGO, policy-making partners and research funding agencies – need to develop a good, pluralistic understanding of the concerns of economy and society. We need to know what matters. This can not only raise awareness but also open up opportunities for the translation of research findings for new and relevant audiences where it can become valuable in use.

2   Invest in models of good, efficacious and ethical research collaboration. Researchers, as a community and as individuals, need to invest in understanding and co-developing models of good, efficacious and ethical collaboration. Developing models of collaboration seems valuable as a way of catalysing action but allowing for the resituating and relearning of what works within and across different settings.

3   Develop dialogic skills. Putting these models into practice requires developing dialogic skills – learning to engage in active listening – being aware of the way language works in a different setting and exploring arresting moments that open up opportunities for imagination, innovation and unfold new ways forward. Developing dialogic skills is critical to reflexivity and also suggests working to establish a flat hierarchy where all forms of knowledge, theoretical and practical are equally valued.

4   Design-in impact to research projects. Collaborative, engaged and action research approaches have been around in business and management for a long time. However, using these approaches as part of large, real-world problem-solution research bids, ensuring that they are well

funded and allow longitudinal study, remains challenging. Yet such approaches enable and resource the fostering of long-term academic-practitioner-policymaker relations such that they become stabilised, trusted and institutionalised, and opening-up new opportunties for HEIs and researchers to really make a difference.

5   Focus on performativity. This focus conceptualises good theorising and good practical knowledge as to sides of the same coin, if one is changed so is the other, across sites of action and across temporalities. This perspective could help make the rigour-relevance arguments of old become irrelevant. A performative approach stands to open up a new focus on where and how researchers work with partners and collaborators and vice versa. Because a performativity lens brings a focus to understanding management learning wherever it happens – in the classroom, through Doctorate of Business Administration (DBAs) with practitioners undertaking doctoral work, or in the field with researchers undertaking managerial work, co-conceptualising, theorising and perhaps sometimes doing business and management – theory purposively applied as an experiment to think and explore the possibilities of change, and in the process reveals how and why adaptations are needed, provoking further theorisation. In this vein, performativity stands to inextricably link research with impact.

Notes

1 www.ref.ac.uk/media/1447/ref-2019_01-guidance-on-submissions.pdf
2 www.ref.ac.uk/media/1450/ref-2019_02-panel-criteria-and-working-methods. pdf
3 https://one.aom.org/one/working-groups/impact-scholar-community
4 https://scholars.org/#
5 www.lancaster.ac.uk/open-valuation/; https://openinnovation.blog.gov.uk/2018/ 01/31/open-innovation-team-deepening-collaboration-between-officials-and-academics/
6 https://behavioralpolicy.org/
7 "large" is a contentious concept in management research. As noted in Chapter 2, the levels of research funding available to management researchers tend to be significantly lower than in other disciplines and the number of staff competing for those awards tends to be higher. In the UK, management represents 8% of all academic staff but attracts only 1% of research funding. It is, therefore, far less common for a mid-career (or indeed, senior) management researcher to have led a substantial research team with a group of post-doctoral researchers, doctoral students and/or research assistants compared to other STEM disciplines. A large award may, therefore, mean a six figure sum which would be seen as relatively modest in other disciplines.

Appendix 6.1

REF2021 impact case study template (from annex g, guidance on submission)

| **Section A** |
| The fields in this section are mandatory. |

| Institution: |

| Unit of Assessment: |

| Title of case study: |

| Period when the underpinning research was undertaken: |

| Details of staff conducting the underpinning research from the submitting unit: |

Name(s):	Role(s) (e.g. job title):	Period(s) employed by submitting HEI:

| Period when the claimed impact occurred: |

| Is this case study continued from a case study submitted! In 2014? Y/N |
| The definition of continued case studies is provided in the "Guidance on submissions", paragraph 316. |

| |

| **Section B** |

| 1. **Summary of the impact** (indicative maximum 100 words) |
| This section should briefly state what specific impact is being described in the case study. |

| 2. **Underpinning research** (indicative maximum 500 words) See paragraphs 318 to 326. This section should outline the key research insights or findings that underpinned the impact and provide details of what research was undertaken, when and by whom. This research may be a body of work produced over a number of years or maybe the output(s) of a particular project. References to specific research outputs that embody the research described in this section, and evidence of its quality, should be provided in the next section (Section B3). |

(*Continued*)

(*Continued*)

Details of the following should be provided in this section:

- The nature of the research insights or findings which relate to the impact claimed in the case study.
- An outline of what the underpinning research produced by the submitted unit was (this may relate to one or more research outputs, projects or programmes).
- Any relevant key contextual information about this area of research.

3. **References to the research** (indicative maximum of six references)

This section should provide references to key outputs from the research described in the previous section and evidence about the quality of the research. Underpinning research outputs may include the full range of types listed in the output glossary (Annex K) and are not limited to printed academic work. All forms of output cited as underpinning research will be considered equitably, with no one type of output being preferred over others.
Include the following details for each cited output:

- authors
- title
- year of publication
- type of output and other relevant details required to identify the output (e.g. DOI or journal title and issue)
- details to enable the panel to gain access to the output, if required (e.g. a DOI or other URL), or stating that the output is listed in REF2 or can be supplied by the HEI on request.

All outputs cited in this section must be capable of being made available to panels. If they are not available in the public domain or listed in REF2, the HEI must be able to provide them if requested by the REF team.

Evidence of the quality of the research must also be provided in this section. Guidance on this is provided in the "Panel criteria".

Where panels request details of key research grants or end of grant reports, the following should be provided:

- who the grant was awarded to
- the grant title
- sponsor
- period of the grant (with dates)
- value of the grant

4. **Details of the impact** (indicative maximum 750 words). The "Panel criteria". Annex A, Table 1 provides an illustrative list of evidence that could be provided.

This section should provide a narrative, with supporting evidence, to explain:

- how the research underpinned (made a distinct and material contribution to) the impact;
- the nature and extent of the impact.

(Continued)

The following should be provided:

- A clear explanation of the process or means through which the research led to, underpinned or made a contribution to the impact (e.g. how it was disseminated, how it came to influence users or beneficiaries or how it came to be exploited, taken up or applied).
- Where the submitted unit's research was part of a wider body of research that contributed to the impact (e.g. where there has been research collaboration with other institutions), the case study should specify the particular contribution of the submitted unit's research and acknowledge other key research contributions.
- Details of the beneficiaries – who or what community, constituency or organisation has benefitted, been affected or impacted on.
- Details of the nature of the impact – how they have benefitted, been affected or impacted on.
- Evidence or indicators of the extent of the impact described, as appropriate to the case being made.
- Dates of when these impacts occurred.

5. **Sources to corroborate the impact** (indicative maximum of ten references) This section should list sources external to the submitting HEI that could, if requested by panels, provide corroboration of specific claims made in the case study. Sources provided in this section should not be *a* substitute for providing clear evidence of impact in Section B4; the information in this section will be used for audit purposes only.

This section should list sufficient sources that could corroborate key claims made about the impact of the unit's research. These could include, as appropriate to the case study, the following external sources of corroboration (stating which claim each source provides corroboration for):

- Reports, reviews, web links or other documented sources of information in the public domain.
- Confidential reports or documents (if listed, these must be submitted to the REF team by 29 January 2021).
- Individual users/beneficiaries who could be contacted by the REF team to corroborate claims*'.
- Factual statements already provided to the HEI by key users/beneficiaries, that corroborate specific claims made in the case study (if listed, these must be submitted to the REF team by 29 January 2021)*.

References

Abend, G. (2008). The meaning of 'theory'. *Sociological Theory*, *26*, 173–199.

Abrahamson, E., Berkowitz, H., & Dumez, H. (2016). A more relevant approach to relevance in management studies: An essay on performativity. *Academy of Management Review*, *41*, 367–381.

Adler, N. J. (2015). Finding beauty in a fractured world: Art inspires leaders: Leaders change the world. *Academy of Management Review*, *40*(3), 480–494.

Aguinis, H., Shapiro, D. L., Antonacopoulou, E. P., & Cummings, T. G. (2014). Scholarly impact: A pluralist conceptualization. *Academy of Management Learning & Education*, *13*(4), 623–639.

Albert, S., & Bartunek, J. M. (2017). Composing a musical score for academic-practitioner collaborative research. In A. Langley & H. Tsoukas (Eds.), *Sage handbook of process organization studies*, pp. 286–302. Los Angeles: Sage.

Anderson, L., Ellwood, P., & Coleman, C. (2017). The impactful academic: Relational management education as an intervention for impact. *British Journal of Management*, *28*(1), 14–28.

Argyris, C. (1996). Crossroads: Unrecognized defenses of scholars: Impact on theory and research. *Organization Science*, *7*(1), 79–87.

Armenakis, A. A., Harris, S. G., & Mossholder, K. W. (1993). Creating readiness for organizational change. *Human Relations*, *46*(6), 681–703.

Aspers, P. (2007). Theory, reality, and performativity in markets. *American Journal of Economics and Sociology*, *66*(2), 379–398.

Astebro, T., Bazzazian, N., & Brguinsky, S. (2012). Startups by recent university graduates and their faculty: Implications for university entrepreneurship policy. *Research Policy*, *41*(4), 663–677.

Aston, E., Murray, K., & O'Neill, M. (2019). Achieving cultural change through organizational justice: The case of stop and search in Scotland. *Criminology & Criminal Justice*, 1748895819839751.

Austin, J. L. (1962). *How to do things with words*. New York: Oxford University Press.

Ayres, I. (1991). Fair driving: Gender and race discrimination in retail car negotiations. *Harvard Law Review*, *104*(4), 817–872.

Barker, R. (2010). No, management is not a profession. *Harvard Business Review*, *88*(7–8), 52–60.

Barley, S. (2016). 60th anniversary issue: Ruminations on how we became a mystery house and how we might get out. *Administrative Science Quarterly, 61*(1), 1–8.44.

Barnes, B. (1983). Social life as bootstrapped induction. *Sociology, 17*(4), 524–545.

Barney, J. 1991. Firm resources and sustained competitive advantage. *Journal of Management, 17*, 99.

Bartunek, J. M. (2007). Academic-practitioner collaboration need not require joint or relevant research: Toward a relational scholarship of integration. *Academy of Management Journal, 50*(6), 1323–1333.

Bartunek, J. M. (2011). Commentary on 'research utilization: Bridging a culture gap between communities' reflecting on research utilization with Janice Beyer. *Journal of Management Inquiry, 20*(4), 392–394.

Bartunek, J. M. (2016). A commentary quiz: What musical composition best describes a primary contribution of your article? *Management Learning, 47*, 100–109.

Bartunek, J. M. (2020). Accomplishing impact by performing our theories: It can be done, though not easily. *Journal of Applied Behavioral Science, 56*(1), 11–31.

Bartunek, J. M., & Louis, M. R. (1996). *Insider-outsider team research.* Thousand Oaks: Sage.

Bartunek, J. M., & McKenzie, J. (Eds.). (2018). *Academic-practitioner relationships: Developments, complexities and opportunities.* Routledge.

Bartunek, J. M., & Moch, M. K. (1987). First-order, second-order, and third-order change and organization development interventions: A cognitive approach. *The Journal of Applied Behavioral Science, 23*(4), 483–500.

Bartunek, J. M., & Rynes, S. L. (2010). The construction and contributions of 'implications for practice': What's in them and what might they offer? *Academy of Management Learning and Education, 9*(1), 100–117.

Bartunek, J. M., & Rynes, S. L. (2014). Academics and practitioners are alike and unlike: The paradoxes of academic-practitioner relationships. *Journal of Management, 40*, 1181–1201.

Bartunek, J. M., & Woodman, R. W. (2015). Beyond Lewin: Toward a temporal approximation of organization development and change. *Annual Review of Organizational Psychology and Organizational Behavior, 2*, 157–182.

Bass, E. (2016). The importance of bringing science and medicine to lay audiences. *Circulation, 133*(23), 2334–2337.

Bastow, S., Dunleavy, P., & Tinkler, J. (2014). *The impact of the social sciences: How academics and their research make a difference.* Los Angeles: Sage.

Bateson, G. (1972). *Steps to an ecology of mind: Collected essays in anthropology, psychiatry, evolution, and epistemology.* Chicago: University of Chicago Press.

Beech, N. (2008). On the nature of dialogic identity work. *Organization, 15*(1), 51–74.

Beech, N. (2017). Identity at work: An enquiry-based approach to therapeutically-inspired management. *International Journal of Management Reviews, 19*(3), 357–370.

Beech, N., & Anseel, F. (2020). COVID-19 and its impact on management research and education: Threats, opportunities, and a manifesto. *British Journal of Management, 31*(4), 447–449.

Beech, N., MacIntosh, R., & MacLean, D. (2010). Dialogues between academics and practitioners: The role of generative dialogic encounters. *Organization Studies*, *31*(9), 1341–1367.

Beech, N., Stewart, D., & Gulledge, E. (2015). Change leadership: The application of alternative models in structural policing changes. In J. Fleming (Ed.), *Police leadership: Rising to the top*, pp. 257–274. Oxford: Oxford University Press.

Beyer, J. M. (1997). Research utilization: Bridging a cultural gap between two communities. *Journal of Management Inquiry*, *6*, 17–22.

Beyer, J. M., & Trice, H. M. (1982). The utilization process: A conceptual framework and synthesis of empirical findings. *Administrative Science Quarterly*, *27*, 591–622.

Bilton, S., & Cummings, S. (2010). *Creative strategy: Reconnecting business and innovation*. Oxford and Hoboken, NJ: Wiley.

Blackler, F. (1993). Knowledge and the theory of organizations: Organizations as activity systems and the reframing of management. *Journal of Management Studies*, *30*(6), 863–884.

Blau, F. D., & Kahn, L. M. (2007). The gender pay gap: Have women gone as far as they can? *Academy of Management Perspectives*, *21*(1), 7–23.

Boudens, C. J. (2005). The story of work: A narrative analysis of workplace emotion. *Organization Studies*, *26*(9), 1285–1306.

Bourdieu, P. (1982). *Ce que parler veut dire: L'économie des échanges linguistiques*. Paris: Fayard. For an English translation, see: Bourdieu, P. (1991). *Language and symbolic power: The economy of linguistic exchange*. Cambridge, MA: Polity.

Boyer, E. L. (1990). *Scholarship reconsidered: Priorities of the professoriate*. Lawrenceville, NJ: Princeton University Press.

Bresnen, M., & Burrell, G. (2013). Journals à la mode? Twenty years of living alongside Mode 2 and the new production of knowledge. *Organization*, *20*(1), 25–37.

Bridgman, T., Cummings, S., & McLaughlin, C. (2016). Restating the case: How revisiting the development of the case method can help us think differently about the future of the business school. *Academy of Management Learning & Education*, *15*(4), 724–741.

Brockbank, A., McGill, I., & Beech, N. (2002). *Reflective learning in practice*. Aldershot: Gower.

Büchel, B., & Antunes, D. (2007). Reflections on executive education: The user and provider's perspectives. *Academy of Management Learning & Education*, *6*(3), 401–411.

Butler, J. (1990). Lana's 'imitation': Melodramatic repetition and the gender performative. *Genders*, (9), 1–18.

Butler, J. (2010). Performative agency. *Journal of Cultural Economy*, *3*(2), 147–161.

Butler, N., Delaney, H., & Spoelstra, S. (2015). Problematizing 'relevance' in the business school: The case of leadership studies. *British Journal of Management*, *26*(4), 731–744.

Callon, M. (1998). *The laws of the markets*. Oxford: Blackwell.

Callon, M. (2009). Elaborating the notion of performativity. *Le libellio d'AEGIS*, *5*(1), 18–29.

Carton, G., & Dameron, S. (2018). How to develop scholar-practitioner interactions: Lessons from management concepts developed through collaboration between research and practice. In J.M. Bartunek & J. McKenzie (Eds.), *Academic-practi tioner relationships: Developments, complexities and opportunities*, pp. 253–270. Routledge.

Cetina, K. K. (2010). The epistemics of information: A consumption model. *Journal of Consumer Culture, 10*(2), 171–201.

Chartered Association of Business Schools. (2020). Research Income for Business and Management:Analysis of HESA data for 2008/09 to 2018/19, May Accessed online May 2020 https://charteredabs.org/wp-content/uploads/2020/05/77403-CABS-Research-Income-Report-2020-WEB-final.pdf

Chia, R., & Holt, R. (2008). The nature of knowledge in business schools. *Academy of Management Learning & Education, 7*, 471–486.

Clarke, N., & Mahadi, N. (2017). Mutual recognition respect between leaders and followers: Its relationship to follower job performance and well-being. *Journal of Business Ethics, 141*, 163–178.

Coch, L., & French Jr., J. R. (1948). Overcoming resistance to change. *Human Relations, 1*(4), 512–532.

Cochoy, F. (1998). Another discipline for the market economy: Marketing as a performative knowledge and know-how for capitalism. *The Sociological Review, 46*(1_suppl), 194–221.

Cochoy, F., Giraudeau, M., & Mcfall, L. (2010). Performativity, economics and politics: An overview. *Journal of Cultural Economy, 3*, 139–146.

Cornuel, E., Thomas, H., & Reed, M. I. (2009). The theory/practice gap: A problem for research in business schools? *Journal of Management Development, 28*, 685–693.

Cook, S., & Seely Brown, J. (1999). Bridging Epistemologies: the generative dance between organizational knowledge and organizational knowing. *Organization Science, 10*(4), 381–400.

Creech, A., Papageorgi, I., Duffy, C., Morton, F., Hadden, E., Potter, J., . . . & Welch, G. (2008). Investigating musical performance: Commonality and diversity among classical and non-classical musicians. *Music Education Research, 10*(2), 215–234.

Crosina, E., & Bartunek, J. M. (2017). The paradoxical mystery of the missing differences between academics and practitioners. In M. Lewis, W. K. Smith, P. Jarzabkowski, & A. Langley (Eds.), *The Oxford handbook of organizational paradox*, pp. 472–489. New York: Oxford.

Cunliffe, A. L. (2002). Reflexive dialogical practice in management learning. *Management Learning, 33*(1), 35–61.

Cunliffe, A. L. (2003). Reflexive inquiry in organizational research: Questions and possibilities. *Human Relations, 56*(8), 983–1003.

Cunliffe, A. L. (2004). On becoming a critically reflexive practitioner. *Journal of Management Education, 28*(4), 407–426..

Currie, G., & Lockett, A. (2007). A critique of transformational leadership: Moral, professional and contingent dimensions of leadership within public services organizations. *Human Relations, 60*(2), 341–370.

Czarniawska, B. (1999). *Writing management: Organization theory as a literary genre*. Oxford: Oxford University Press.

Davis, G. F. (2015). Editorial essay: What is organizational research for? *Administrative Science Quarterly*, *60*(2), 179–188.

Delbridge, R. (2014). Promising futures: CMS, post-disciplinarity and the new public social science. *Journal of Management Studies*, *51*, 95–117.

Derrida, J. (1991). Signature event context. In P. Kamuf (Ed.), *A Derrida reader: Between the blinds*. New York: Columbia University Press.

Dewey, J. (1933). Analysis of reflective thinking. In L. Hickman & T. M. Alexander (Eds.), *The essential Dewey: Ethics, logic, psychology*. Bloomington: Indiana University Press.

Dewey, J. (1938). *Logic: The theory of inquiry*. New York: Holt and London: Allen & Unwin.

Dickinson, D. (2016). Behind the scenes: Creative commons publishing. *The conversation* (29 October), https://theconversation.com/behind-the-scenes-creative-commons-publishing-67375

Drennan, D. (1992). *Transforming Company Culture*. London: McGraw-Hill.

Dunne, J. (2005). An intricate fabric: Understanding the rationality of practice. *Pedagogy, Culture & Society*, *13*(3), 367–390.

Eden, C., & Huxham, C. (1996). Action research for management research. *British Journal of Management*, *7*(1), 75–86.

Eisenhardt K.M. and Martin A. (2000). Dynamic capabilities: what are they? *Strategic Management Journal, 21*(10–11), 1105–1121.

Empson, L. (2013). My affair with the 'other': Identity journeys across the research-practice divide. *Journal of Management Inquiry*, *22*(2), 229–248.

Engwall, L., & Kipping, M. (2004). Introduction: The dissemination of management knowledge. *Management Learning*, *35*, 243–253.

Etzion, D., & Gehman, J. (2019). Going public: Debating matters of concern as an imperative for management scholars. *Academy of Management Review*, *44*, 480–492.

Fletcher, I. (2010). Dubious assumptions of the theory of comparative advantage. *Real-World Economics Review*, *54*, 94–105.

Fournier, V., & Grey, C. (2000). At the critical moment: Conditions and prospects for critical management studies. *Human Relations*, *53*, 7–32.

Gabor, E. (2013). Tuning the body of the classical musician. *Qualitative Research in Organizations and Management*, *8*(3), 206–223.

Gergen, K. J. (2009). *Relational being: Beyond self and community*. Oxford: Oxford University Press.

Gergen, K. J., Gergen, M. M., & Barrett, F. J. (2004). Dialogue: Life and death of the organization. In D. Grant, C. Hardy, C. Oswick, & L. Putnam (Eds.), *The Sage handbook of organizational discourse*, pp. 39–59. London: Sage.

Gherardi, S. (2000). Practice-based theorizing on learning and knowing in organizations. *Organization*, *7*(2), 211–223.

Gherardi, S. (2006). *Organizational knowledge: The texture of workplace learning*. Oxford: Blackwell Publishing.

Gherardi, S. (2009). Introduction: The critical power of the 'practice lens'. *Management Learning*, *40*(2), 115–128.

Ghoshal, S. (2005). Bad management theories are destroying good management practices. *Academy of Management Learning & Education*, *4*(1), 75–91.

Gibbons, M., Limoges, C., Nowotny, H., & Schwartzman, S. (1994). *The new production of knowledge: The dynamics of science and research in contemporary societies*. London: Sage.

Goffman, E. (1958). *The presentation of self in everyday life*. Harmondsworth: Penguin.

Goffman, E. (1974). *Frame analysis: An essay on the organization of experience*. Cambridge, MA: Harvard University Press.

Gond, J. P., Cabantous, L., Harding, N., & Learmonth, M. (2016). What do we mean by performativity in organizational and management theory? The uses and abuses of performativity. *International Journal of Management Reviews*, *18*(4), 440–463.

Greig, G., Entwistle, V. A., & Beech, N. (2012a). Addressing complex healthcare problems in diverse settings: Insights from activity theory. *Social Science and Medicine*, *74*, 305–312.

Greig, G., Gilmore, C., Patrick, H., & Beech, N. (2012b). Arresting moments in engaged management research. *Management Learning*, *44*(3), 267–285.

Griffiths, W. (2011). Fuel from waste, www.youtube.com/user/Fuelfromwaste

Hamet, J., & Maurer, F. (2017). Is management research visible outside the academic community? *Management*, *20*(5), 492–516.

Harraway, D. (1988). Situated knowledge: The science question in feminism and the privilege of partial perspective. *Feminist Studies*, *14*, 575–599.

Hassard, J., & Kelemen, M. (2002). Production and consumption in organizational knowledge: The case of the 'paradigms debate'. *Organization*, *9*(2), 331–355.

Heusinkveld, S., Sturdy, A., & Werr, A. (2011). The co-consumption of management ideas and practices. *Management Learning*, *42*(2), 139–147.

Hibbert, P., Coupland, C., & MacIntosh, R. (2010). Reflexivity: Recursion and relationality in organizational research processes. *Qualitative Research in Organizations and Management: An International Journal*, *5*(1), 47–62.

Huber, A. (2018). Design research: Off the rails or on the right track? *Design Management Journal*, *12*(1), 40–55.

Hunt, S. D. (2002). Marketing as a profession: On closing stakeholder gaps. *European Journal of Marketing*, *36*, 305–312.

Isaacs, W. (1993). Taking flight: Dialogue, collective thinking and organizational learning. *Organizational Dynamics*, *22*, 24–39.

Isaacs, W. (1999). *Dialogue: The art of thinking together*. New York: Doubleday.

Jaworski, B. J. (2011). On managerial relevance. *Journal of Marketing*, *75*, 211–224.

Kamoche, K., & Cunha, M. (2001). Minimal structures: From jazz improvization to product innovation. *Organisation Studies*, *22*(5), 733–764.

Kanter, R. M. (2005). What theories do audiences want? Exploring the demand side. *Academy of Management Learning & Education*, *4*(1), 93–95.

Keating, A., Geiger, S., & McLoughlin, D. (2014). Riding the practice waves: Social resourcing practices during new venture development. *Entrepreneurship Theory and Practice*, *38*(5), 1–29.

Kelemen, M., & Bansal, P. (2002). The conventions of management research and their relevance to management practice. *British Journal of Management*, *13*(2), 97–108.

Khurana, R., & Nohria, N. (2008). It's time to make management a true profession. *Harvard Business Review*, *86*(10), 70–77.

Kieser, A., & Leiner, L. (2009). Why the rigour-relevance gap in management research is unbridgeable. *Journal of Management Studies*, *46*(3), 516–533.

King, D., & Learmonth, M. (2015). Can critical management studies ever be 'practical'? A case study in engaged scholarship. *Human Relations*, *68*(3), 353–375.

Kjellberg, H., & Helgesson, C. F. (2006). Multiple versions of markets: Multiplicity and performativity in market practice. *Industrial Marketing Management*, *35*(7), 839–855.

Knights, D., & Clarke, C. A. (2014). It's a bittersweet symphony, this life: Fragile academic selves and insecure identities at work. *Organization Studies*, *35*(3), 335–357.

Kurkoski, J. (2018). Applied R&D in HR: Google's People Innovation Lab. In J.M. Bartunek & J. McKenzie (Eds.), *Academic-practitioner relationships: Developments, complexities and opportunities*, pp. 312–323. Routledge.

Landman, T., Glowinkowski, S., & Demes, K. (2018). Making values matter: An academic and private sector collaboration. In J.M. Bartunek & J. McKenzie (Eds.), *Academic-practitioner relationships: Developments, complexities and opportunities*, pp. 271–290. Routledge.

Lambert, D. M., & Enz, M. G. (2015). We must find the courage to change. *Journal of Business Logistics*, *36*(1), 9–17.

Lambrechts, F. J., Bouwen, R., Grieten, S., Huybrechts, J. P., & Schein, E. H. (2011). Learning to help through humble inquiry and implications for management research, practice, and education: An interview with Edgar H. Schein. *Academy of Management Learning & Education*, *10*(1), 131–147.

Latour, B. (1986). The powers of association. In J. Law (Ed.), *Power, action and belief: A new sociology of knowledge*. London: Routledge & Kegan Paul.

Lavine, M. (2014). Paradoxical leadership and the competing values framework. *Journal of Applied Behavioral Science*, *50*(2), 189–205.

Law, J. (2004). Matter-ing: Or how might STS contribute? Centre for Science Studies, Lancaster University, Lancaster LA1 4YL, UK, www.comp.lancs.ac.uk/sociology/papers/law-matter-ing.pdf

Lewin, K. (1947). Frontiers in Group Dynamics, concept method and reality in social science; social equilibria and social change. *Human Relations*, I, 2–38.

Leyser, O. (2020). Viewpoint: We must reshape the system to value and support difference, www.ukri.org/news/viewpoint-we-must-reshape-the-system-so-it-genuinely-values-and-supports-difference/

Lowenstein, R. (2000). *When genius failed: The rise and fall of long-term capital management*. New York: Random House Trade Paperbacks.

Lynch, J., Bennett, D., Luntz, A., Toy, C., & Van Benschoten, E. (2014). Bridging science and journalism: Identifying the role of public relations in the construction and circulation of stem cell research among laypeople. *Science Communication*, *36*(4), 479–501.

Lyotard, J.-F. (1979). *The postmodern condition: A report on knowledge*. Manchester: Manchester University Press.

MacIntosh, R., Bartunek, J., Bhatt, M., & MacLean, D. (2016). I never promised you a rose garden: Reflections on the evolution of research questions. In A. B.

Shani & D. Mouair (Eds.), *Research in organizational change and development*, vol. 24, pp. 47–82. Bingley: Emerald.

MacIntosh, R., Beech, N., Antonacopoulou, E., & Sims, D. (2012). Practising and knowing management: A dialogic perspective. *Management Learning*, *43*(4), 373–383.

MacIntosh, R., Beech, N., Bartunek, J., Mason, K., Cooke, W., & Denyer, D. (2017). Impact and management research: Exploring relationships between temporality, dialogue, reflexivity and praxis. *British Journal of Management*, *28*(1), 3–13.

MacIntosh, R., Beech, N., & Martin, G. (2012). Dialogues and dialetics: Limits to clinician-manager interaction in healthcare organizations. *Social Science and Medicine*, *74*(3), 332–339.

MacKenzie, D. (2006). *An engine, not a camera: How financial models shape markets*. Boston: MIT Press.

MacKenzie, D. (2007). Is economics performative? In D. A. MacKenzie, F. Muniesa, & L. Siu (Eds.), *Do economists make markets? On the performativity of economics*, pp. 54–86. Princeton, NJ: Princeton University Press.

Maclaran, P., Miller, C., Parsons, E., & Surman, E. (2009). Praxis or performance: Does critical marketing have a gender blind-spot? *Journal of Marketing Management*, *25*(7–8), 713–728.

MacLean, D., MacIntosh, R., & Grant, S. (2002). Mode 2 management research. *British Journal of Management*, *13*(3), 189–207.

Markides, C. (2011). Crossing the chasm: How to convert relevant research into managerially useful research. *Journal of Applied Behavioral Science*, *47*(1), 121–134.

Marks, M. L., Mirvis, P., & Ashkenas, R. (2017). Surviving M&A how to thrive amid the turmoil. *Harvard Business Review*, *95*(2), 145–150.

Mason, K. (2012). Market sensing and situated dialogic action research (with a video camera). *Management Learning*, *43*(4), 405–425.

Mason, K., & Araujo, L. (2020). Implementing marketization in public healthcare systems: Performing reform in the English National Health Service. *British Journal of Management*, https://doi.org/10.1111/1467-8551.12417

Mason, K., Friesl, M., & Ford, C. J. (2017). Managing to make markets: Marketization and the conceptualization work of strategic nets in the life science sector. *Industrial Marketing Management*, *67*, 52–69.

Mason, K., Friesl, M., & Ford, C. J. (2019). Markets under the microscope: Making scientific discoveries valuable through choreographed contestations. *Journal of Management Studies*, *56*(5), 966–999.

Mason, K., Kjellberg, H., & Hagberg, J. (2015). Exploring the performativity of marketing: Theories, practices and devices. *Journal of Marketing Management*, *31*(1–2), 1–15.

Mason, K., & Spring, M. (2011). The sites and practices of business models. *Industrial Marketing Management*, *40*(6), 1032–1041.

McCloskey, D. (1998). *The rhetoric of economics*. Madison, WI: University of Wisconsin Press.

McKenzie, J., van Winkelen, C., & Bartunek, J. M. (2014). *Elaborating from practice on the theoretical model of engaged scholarship*. Philadelphia: Academy of Management Meeting.

Millerson, G. (1964). *The qualifying associations: a study in professionalization.* London: Routledge & Kegan Paul.

Mohrman, S. A. (2018). Partnering to advance sustainable effectiveness at the Center for Effective Organizations. In J. M. Bartunek & J. McKenzie (Eds.), *Academic-practitioner relationships: Developments, complexities and opportunities*, pp. 217–233. New York: Routledge.

Muniesa, F., & Callon, M. (2007). Economic experiments and the construction of markets. In D. A. MacKenzie, F. Muniesa, & L. Siu (Eds.), *Do economists make markets? On the performativity of economics.* Princeton, NJ: Princeton University Press.

Nguyen, T., & Janssens, M. (2019). Knowledge, emotion, and power in social partnership: A turn to partners' context. *Organization Studies*, *40*(3), 371–393.

Nicolini, D. (2012). *Practice theory, work and organization.* Oxford: Oxford University Press.

Nobel, C. (2016). Why isn't business research more relevant to business practitioners? *Harvard Business School working knowledge* (19 September), http://hbswk.hbs.edu

Palo, T., Mason, K., & Roscoe, P. (2020). Performing a myth to make a market: The construction of the 'magical world' of Santa. *Organization Studies*, *41*(1), 53–75.

Patriotta, G. (2016). Cities of noise: A brief inquiry into sensemaking, sensemakers and organized worlds. *Academy of Management Review*, *41*, 557–570.

Pelz, D. C. (1978). Some expanded perspectives on use of social science in public policy. In M. Yinger & S. J. Cutler (Eds.), *Major social issues: A multidisciplinary view*, pp. 346–357. New York, NY: Free Press.

Perkmann, M., & Walsh, K. (2008). Engaging the scholar: Three forms of academic consulting and their impact on universities and industry. *Research Policy*, *37*, 1884–1891.

Peters, T. J., & Waterman, R. H. (1982). *In search of excellence: Lessons from America's best-run companies.* New York: Harper and Row.

Peterson, C. L. (2016). Consumer Financial Protection Bureau law enforcement: An empirical review. *Tulane Law Review, 90*, 1057–1112.

Pettigrew, A. M. (1997). The double hurdles for management research. In T. Clarke (Ed.), *Advancement in organizational behaviour: Essays in honour of D. S. Pugh*, pp. 277–296. London: Dartmouth.

Pettigrew, A. M. (2001). Management research after modernism. *British Journal of Management*, *12*, 61–70.

Pettigrew, A. P. (2011). Scholarship with impact. *British Journal of Management*, *22*, 347–354.

Pfeffer, J. (2005). Why do bad management theories persist? A comment on Ghoshal. *Academy of Management Learning & Education*, *4*(1), 96–100.

Pfeffer, J., & Fong, C. T. (2002). The end of business schools? Less success than meets the eye. *Academy of Management Learning and Education*, *1*(1), 78–95.

Ployhart, R. E., & Bartunek, J. M. (2019). Editors' comments: There is nothing so theoretical as good practice: A call for phenomenal theory. *Academy of Management Review*, *44*, 493–497.

Porter, M. E. (1980). *Competitive strategy*. New York, NY: Free Press.

Ragin, C. C., & Becker, H. S. (Eds.). (1992). *What is a case?: Exploring the foundations of social inquiry*. Cambridge: Cambridge University Press.

Ren, I. Y., & Bartunek, J. M. (2020). Creating standards for responsible translation of management research for practitioners. In O. Laasch, R. Suddaby, R. E. Freeman, & D. Jamali (Eds.), *Research handbook of responsible management*, pp. 729–744. Cheltenham, England: Edward Elgar.

Rescher, N. (1996). *Process metaphysics: An introduction to process philosophy*. Albany, NY: State University of New York Press.

Romme, A. G. L., Avenier, M., Denyer, D., Hodgkinson, G. P., Pandza, K., Starkey, K., & Worren, N. (2015). Towards common ground and trading zones in management research and practice. *British Journal of Management, 26,* 544–559.

Rynes, S. L., McNatt, D. B., & Bretz, R. D. (1999). Academic research inside organizations: Inputs, processes, and outcomes. *Personnel Psychology, 52*(4), 869–898.

Sandelands, L. E. (1990). What is so practical about theory? Lewin revisited. *Journal for the Theory of Social Behavior, 20*(3), 235–262.

Schaffer, F. C. (2016). *Elucidating Social Science Concepts: an Interpretive Guide*. New York: Routledge.

Schein, E. H. (2020). Social scientists need to speak up. Unpublished document.

Schön, D. A. (1983). *The reflective practitioner: How professionals think in action*. New York: Basic Books.

Schwitzer, G., Mudur, G., Henry, D., Wilson, A., Goozner, M., Simbra, M., Sweet, M., & Baverstock, K. A. (2005). What are the roles and responsibilities of the media in disseminating health information? *PLoS Medicine, 2*(7), e321.

Sealy, Ruth, et al. (2017). Expanding the notion of dialogic trading zones for impactful research: The case of women on boards research. *British Journal of Management, 28*(1), 64–83.

Segon, M., Booth, C., & Pearce, J. (2019). Management as a profession: A typology based assessment. *Management Decision, 57*(9), 2177–2200.

Senge, P. (1990). *The fifth discipline: The art and practice of the learning organization*. New York: Doubleday.

Shotter, J. (2006). Understanding Process From Within: An Argument for 'Withness'-Thinking. *Organization Studies, 27*(4), 585–604.

Shotter, J., & Tsoukas, H. (2011). Theory as therapy: Wittgensteinian reminders for reflective theorizing in organization and management theory. *Research in the Sociology of Organizations, 32,* 311–342.

Spicer, A., Alvesson, M., & Kärreman, D. (2009). Critical performativity: The unfinished business of critical management studies. *Human Relations, 62*(4), 537–560.

Starkey, K., & Madan, P. (2001). Bridging the relevance gap: Aligning stakeholders in the future of management research. *British Journal of Management, 12,* 3–26.

Styhre, A. (2016). What David Foster Wallace can teach management scholars. *Academy of Management Review, 41*(1), 170–183.

Susman, G. I., & Evered, R. D. (1978). An assessment of the scientific merits of action research. *Administrative Science Quarterly, 23,* 582–603.

Tadajewski, M. (2010). Critical marketing studies: Logical empiricism, 'critical performativity' and marketing practice. *Marketing Theory*, *10*(2), 210–222.

Teece, D.J., Pisano, G. and Shuen, A. (1997). Dynamic capabilities and strategic management. *Strategic Management Journal*, *18*(7), 509–533.

Thorpe, R., Eden, C., Bessant, J., & Ellwood, P. (2011). Rigour, relevance and reward: Introducing the knowledge translation value chain. *British Journal of Management*, *22*, 420–431.

Times Higher Education. (2020). World university rankings methodology, www.timeshighereducation.com/world-university-rankings/world-university-rankings-2020-methodology

Tourish, D. (2019). *Management studies in crisis: Fraud, deception and meaningless research.* Cambridge: Cambridge University Press.

Tranfield, D., & Starkey, K. (1998). The nature, social organization and promotion of management research: Towards policy. *British Journal of Management*, *9*(4), 341–353.

Troth, A., Lawrence, S., Jordan, P., & Ashkanasy, N. (2018). Interpersonal emotion regulation in the workplace: A conceptual and operational review and future research agenda. *International Journal of Management Reviews*, *20*, 523–543.

Tsoukas, H. (2019). *Philosophical organization theory.* Oxford, USA: Oxford University Press.

Tushman, M. L., O'Reilly, C., Fenollosa, A., Kleinbaum, A. M., & McGrath, D. (2007). Relevance and rigor: Executive education as a lever in shaping practice and research. *Academy of Management Learning & Education*, *6*(3), 345–362.

Usher, R., Bryant, I., & Johnston, R. (1997). *Adult education and the postmodern challenge: Learning beyond the limits.* London, GBR and Florence, KY: Routledge.

Van de Ven, A. H. (2007). *Engaged scholarship: A guide for organizational and social research.* New York: Oxford University Press.

Vaughan, D. (2014). Analogy, Cases and Comparative Social Organization. In R. Swedberg (Ed.), *Theorizing in Social Science: The Context of Discovery,* pp.61–84. Stanford, California: Stanford University Press.

Wagenaar, H. (2004). 'Knowing' the rules: Administrative work as practice. *Public Administration Review*, *64*(6), 643–656.

Wasserman, I. C., & Kram, K. E. (2009). Enacting the scholar: Practitioner role: An exploration of narratives. *Journal of Applied Behavioral Science*, *45*(1), 12–38.

Weick, K. E. (1989). Theory construction as disciplined imagination. *Academy of Management Review*, *14*(4), 516–531.

Weiss, C. H., & Bucuvalas, M. J. (1977). The challenge of social research to decision making. In C. H. Weiss (Ed.), *Using social research in public policy making,* pp. 213–234. Lexington: Lexington Books.

Whiteman, G., & Cooper, W. H. (2016). Decoupling rape. *Academy of Management Discoveries*, *2*(2), 115–154.

Wieviorka, M. (1992). Case studies: History or sociology. In C. C. Ragin & H. S. Becker (Eds.), *What is a case? Exploring the foundations of social inquiry.* Cambridge, GBR: Cambridge University Press.

Wilhelm, H., & Bort, S. (2013). How managers talk about their consumption of popular management concepts: Identity, rules and situations. *British Journal of Management*, *24*(3), 428–444.

Wittgenstein, L. (1953). *Philosophical investigations* (trans. G. E. M. Anscombe). Oxford: Blackwell.

Wright, R. P., Paroutis, S. E., & Blettner, D. P. (2013). How useful are the strategic tools we teach in business schools? *Journal of Management Studies, 50*(1), 92–125.

Zwick, D., & Cayla, J. (Eds.). (2011). *Inside marketing: Practices, ideologies, devices.* Oxford: Oxford University Press.

Index

Note: Page numbers in *italic* indicate a figure and page numbers in **bold** indicate a table on the corresponding page.